RECOVERY

from

COMPULSIVE

EATING

*A Complete Guide to The
Twelve Step Program*

Jim A.

HAZELDEN

Hazelden Educational Materials
Center City, Minnesota 55012-0176

Library of Congress Cataloging in Publication Data
A., Jim.
    Recovery from compulsive eating : a complete guide to the twelve step program / Jim A.
        p.   cm.
    Includes index.
    ISBN 1-56838-017-8
    1. Compulsive eaters--Rehabilitation. 2. Twelve-step programs.
I. Title.
RC552.C65A23   1994
616.86'26--dc20   93-45762
                                                                          CIP

Editor's note
Hazelden Educational Materials offers a variety of information on chemical dependency and related areas. Our publications do not necessarily represent Hazelden's programs, nor do they officially speak for any Twelve Step organization.

The Twelve Steps and the Twelve Traditions of AA are reprinted with permission of Alcoholics Anonymous World Services, Inc. Permission to reprint the Twelve Steps and the Twelve Traditions of Alcoholics Anonymous does not mean that Alcoholics Anonymous has reviewed or approved the contents of this publication, nor that AA agrees with the views expressed herein. The views expressed here are solely those of the author. AA is a program of recovery from alcoholism. Use of the Twelve Steps in connection with programs and activities that are patterned after AA but which address other problems does not imply otherwise.

Permission to use the Twelve Steps of Alcoholics Anonymous and the Twelve Traditions of Alcoholics Anonymous for adaptation granted to Overeaters Anonymous by AA World Services, Inc. The Twelve Steps of Overeaters Anonymous and the Twelve Traditions of Overeaters Anonymous, as adapted, are reprinted here with the permission of Overeaters Anonymous, Inc. Permission to reprint OA's Twelve Steps does not mean that OA has reviewed or approved the content of this publication, nor that OA agrees with the views expressed herein.

The following publisher has generously given permission to use extended quotations from a copyrighted work: From the *Diagnostic and Statistical Manual of Mental Disorders,* 3d ed., revised (DSM-III-R) ©1987 American Psychiatric Association.

Acquisitions Editor: Timothy Quinn McIndoo
Manuscript Editor: Debora O'Donnell-Tavolier
Cover design: David Spohn
Interior design: Timothy Quinn McIndoo
Typographer: Deborah Wischow
Copywriter: Tina Petersen
Print Manager: Joan Siem
Printer: Versa Press, Inc.
Production Editor: Cynthia Madsen
Indexer: Holly Biggins
Managing Editor: Donald H. Freeman
This book is printed in Adobe Garamond

Contents

Preface

Overeaters Anonymous has taken 110 pounds off my body and kept it off since 1982. This is a miracle, since I had never been thin before in my life. In OA, one way we keep off our excess weight is to help other overeaters who want to recover. Writing this book has been one way for me to do that.

This book isn't just another "How I Lost Weight" book, since it doesn't advocate a particular diet; nor is it based on my theories alone. It's not a theoretical book but a practical one based heavily on my own experience and that of over 150,000 men and women in OA around the world. This book is a guide, not a gospel; it reflects my views only and not necessarily those of OA as a whole.

Recovery from Compulsive Eating is a complete reference to recovering from compulsive eating through OA. It covers everything from getting started and figuring out what to eat to working the steps of recovery. Even though OA publishes several good books and pamphlets, it still relies heavily on Alcoholics Anonymous literature. The result is that what you really need to know is scattered through the pages of many different books and pamphlets. *Recovery from Compulsive Eating* gathers the information about the program and puts it in one place for the first time.

This book is intended to serve a number of audiences. Anyone who wants to lose weight and keep it off will benefit from this book. Although OA isn't a diet club, losing excess weight is one of the important fringe benefits of working the program. I have done my best to document precisely what works in OA for long-term success. Even if you aren't a member of OA, you can learn numerous useful techniques for getting through a day without overeating. For example, the description of the nature of our food problems may give you insight into your own problems. There are also sections on how to enjoy tricky occasions, such as trips and parties, without overeating. Other topics include how to deal with your family and other close relationships.

Those who have made a decision to try OA and who want a little more guidance will find this book especially useful. It takes a while to "get" the program, since it's not a diet club and yet much more than a support group. The book talks candidly about exactly what does and doesn't work for the long term. It contains a lot of the unwritten lore of the OA program that's passed on from one recovering overeater to another. It tells you almost everything you need to know to get started on a good recovery.

The book is also intended for the friends and family members of overeaters. Perhaps it will give them some insight into what eating disorders are really like. I have included special sections for parents and partners so that they can understand what we are going through and perhaps be more effective in helping us get better.

Recovery from Compulsive Eating can help those who wonder whether they should join OA. It describes the OA program in extensive detail so that an informed decision can be made. Many people get a distorted view of the program through secondhand reports from well-meaning, but perhaps misinformed, acquaintances. There is a lot more to OA than meets the eye. Rather than writing a rah-rah book that tries to push OA for everyone, I make it clear who might benefit from OA and who might not.

Not all who have trouble with overeating need to lose weight. For example, many overeaters have used dangerous methods such as vomiting, starving, or taking laxatives to control their weight. The methods we use for relieving our eating compulsion in OA can work for them as well.

Anyone interested in the study of eating disorders or weight control, including physicians, researchers, nutritionists, therapists, and counselors, should find this book useful. *Recovery from Compulsive Eating* describes what the fellowship of OA has to offer, its strengths as well as its weaknesses, and how it can supplement other forms of treatment. Special sections are addressed to doctors and researchers to help them better understand what overeaters have been going through.

The book begins with an overview of what OA is and isn't and then discusses the basic philosophy behind the program. Several sections are devoted to how to get better, paying particular attention to the phases we progress through and what happens after we lose the weight. The Twelve Steps and Twelve Traditions, which are the core of OA, are discussed in detail. Finally, the book offers advice on how to prevent and recover from relapse.

After talking about some things over and over again in OA, we have developed a kind of shorthand, whether it's "turning over a Fourth Step" or arguing about H.O.W. meetings. I have done my best to keep the jargon to a minimum, but I have included a glossary at the back of this book to help you understand the language.

Let me add another note about language. As one who believes in equal rights for all, I tried to use nonsexist language in writing this book. Please bear with me if some of the results seem awkward: "I" refers to my own experience, and the plural "we" refers to things that I believe are generally agreed upon in OA. However, I don't speak for OA as a whole; no one does. I am just another OA member sharing my own experiences about how I recovered from overeating.

This isn't an official OA publication. It's neither endorsed nor opposed by Overeaters Anonymous, Inc. I chose to publish this work outside of OA because I wanted the freedom to discuss some matters that are rather touchy within the fellowship and unlikely to be discussed candidly for a long time in the official literature. For example, in 1986 OA stopped publishing food plans for a variety of good reasons. But there had been bitter infighting over food plans for years. OA now appears to be reluctant to publish anything specific about what to eat because it might be seen as a return to food plans. I have tried to speak candidly, without being dogmatic, about how we eat in recovery.

I don't expect anyone to agree with everything that I have written, but I hope that this book is useful to everyone who reads it. As we say in the fellowship, "Take what you need and leave the rest."

Acknowledgments

In writing this book, I owe a great deal to a lot of people, and there is no way I can properly thank all of them. Some of them, however, deserve special mention. Overeaters Anonymous would be nowhere without the experience of Alcoholics Anonymous. Bill W., Dr. Bob, and thousands of other AAs have shown by their example that it's possible to overcome addiction. I also owe a tremendous debt to the thousands of men and women in OA who saved my life and made my recovery from obesity possible, including Rozanne S. and the other pioneers of OA, without whom this book wouldn't be possible.

A number of people in OA have gone out of their way to help me and thus deserve special mention, but the list would go on for pages, so I will name just a few: Gwen, Frank, Charles, Anne, Eliot, Beth, Dennis, Dan, Vic, and Frank. Many others have inspired me through their examples: Irene, Bill, and Fred, to name a few.

I also owe a special debt of gratitude for those in the media who let me know about OA, including D. Keith Mano, Dear Abby, Ann Landers, and Stella Barber.

I want to say a special thank-you to those who read the drafts of this book and made so many good suggestions for its improvement. My editor at Hazelden, Tim McIndoo, has been especially helpful with suggestions for improving the draft. I owe special thanks to my thesis advisor for not torturing me for taking the time away from my dissertation to write this book.

I also wish to acknowledge the love and support of my family, who had no idea what to do with the food addict living in their midst. Their support through fat and thin, not to mention high water, was invaluable. And last but not least, my wife Amy deserves lots and lots of hugs.

I
Getting Started

We have learned that the reasons are unimportant. What deserves the attention of the still-suffering compulsive overeater is this: *there is a proven, workable method by which we can arrest our illness.*
—*Overeaters Anonymous*
(The Brown Book)

My story

We in Overeaters Anonymous are beating the odds. Statistics say that diets fail and that people who lose weight almost always gain it back. And yet many of us have managed to lose weight and keep it off. We are the veterans of countless battles against our fat, and most times we lost. We tried diets, shots, pills, health clubs, and therapists. Then we tried even more diets, and still we couldn't conquer the fat. We are the dropouts and flunk-outs of every weight and food control program imaginable. Many of us thought we were doomed to be fat for the rest of our lives.

How can a bunch of the most hopeless fat people like us manage to lose weight, keep it off, and stay sane in the process? We do it by following the suggested program of OA, which uses the successful principles of Alcoholics Anonymous.

My own story is somewhat typical. I couldn't go on living the way I was, twenty-two years old and 110 pounds overweight. Another attempt at a geographic cure for my obesity had failed, and I found myself living in a strange city thousands of miles from home.

With no friends and not knowing how to make friends, my days consisted of getting up, eating junk food, going to work, and then eating more junk food when I got home. Even though I didn't know anyone on my street, I still would close the curtains in my apartment so that no one could see the way I ate. As if they couldn't tell that I ate too much from looking at my forty-six-inch waist! The pants I had bought at the "big and tall" shop had worn through in the crotch in less than six weeks and were already tight on me. Climbing steps was an ordeal; my blood pressure was climbing as well. And then there were those nights when I would have chest pains and not know if I was going to wake up the next day. I had to do something, but I didn't know what.

I had tried a variety of potential solutions over the years. I went on my first diet when I was ten and lost about thirty pounds, which was about half of what I needed to lose at the time. I quickly gained it back. There were several other diets, but I was unable to stick to them. Needless to say, I went through all the usual crap that a fat kid goes through in a fat-phobic society, but I need not dwell on that here. I thought the weight was obviously my parents' fault, so when I was eighteen I tried a geographic cure and moved to California. But I took my eating disorder with me and continued to gain weight. Neither a stint with my college football team nor health food fixed me. I tried moving from Southern California to Northern California, but my eating got worse than ever.

Somewhere in the back of my head I remembered the words "Overeaters Anonymous." I had heard about them for years. I looked up OA in the phone book; my heart pounded as I dialed the number.

I had no idea what to expect. Was it some kind of fat club that would teach me to accept myself and give me the comradeship of other fat people? I had read about such clubs, but had always been too disgusted by my own fat to want to be around other fat people. Was it a fat-liberation group that would campaign for our civil rights and fight the massive amount of weight-based discrimination in our thin-worshipping society? Was it a bunch of Holy Rollers? Or was this the diet club that put you in the pigpen if you gained weight that week?

I hoped the line would be busy. It wasn't, but a machine answered. Whew! At least I could find out something without their thinking that I was fat! An articulate male voice with the trace of an English accent told me that OA was a fellowship of men and women, that there were no dues or fees, and that OA was not allied with any religious sect or denomination. The voice then told me the location of several meetings. It took me another month before I gathered enough courage—or, rather, became desperate enough—to waddle into my first meeting.

Since that time, I have made my recovery from compulsive overeating a top priority in my life, having attended hundreds of OA meetings in several states and four countries. Through the help of OA, I lost that 110 pounds and have been maintaining my goal weight for over ten years.

What is OA?

❦ An overview

You may have a lot of fear about trying OA. You may think it will humiliate you like some other diet clubs, bankrupt you, or make you loony. Let me reassure you.

We aren't a diet club and we don't have mandatory food plans or weigh-ins. There are no weight restrictions on membership. Indeed, as is usually stated at meetings, "the only requirement for membership is a desire to stop eating compulsively."

We don't endorse, oppose, or affiliate with any outside enterprises. Thus, there is no official OA diet food or OA resort. We don't espouse any religious doctrine. We unashamedly adapt the principles of Alcoholics Anonymous because we have discovered that those principles also work for compulsive overeating.

We help ourselves by helping other overeaters. A lot of this is done at meetings where we share with each other what does and doesn't work for us. There are now over ten thousand OA meetings around the world.

OA is inexpensive. Nobody has to pay any dues or fees to attend OA meetings, so you need not worry about being able to afford it. We pass the hat to pay for expenses, but contributions are completely voluntary, and no one keeps track of who gives what.

❦ This is the last house on the block

For many of us, OA is the last house on the block. Collectively, we have tried and failed at just about every other means of controlling our weight and our eating. We have dieted and lost weight only to gain it all back and more. We have joined spas and health clubs. We have gone to fat farms. We have spent thousands of dollars on legal and illegal drugs. We have gone to diet doctors, shot doctors, and therapists of every type. We have tried fasting, vomiting, laxatives, and exercise. We have tried moving to different locations to leave our problems behind, and we have tried returning home. We have had staples put in our stomachs as well as our ears. We have had our intestines bypassed and our jaws wired.[*] We have had ourselves injected

---

[*]Intestinal bypass surgery had a high complication rate and has been for the most part superseded by gastroplasty (stomach stapling). Jaw wiring is not often done for weight-loss purposes because of the danger of asphyxiation if the patient vomits.

with substances from the urine of pregnant women.* We have had balloons implanted in our stomachs, submitted ourselves to electric shocks, and we tried still more diets.

We are the veterans of Stillman, Atkins, Beverly Hills, Grapefruit, Air Force, Drinking Man's, and Liquid Protein diets, as well as countless commercial diet clubs. We have tried using smaller plates, always putting our fork down between bites, and chewing each bite twenty times. We have tried never eating in front of the TV, never eating standing up, and never eating sitting down. We have tried writing down what we planned to eat, and what we had already eaten. We have tried health food and started bingeing on that as well.

We had good incentives to lose weight. Relatives would try to bribe us with money and clothes, but we couldn't keep the weight off. Even our own poor health was not enough; we knew that the food and weight were killing us, but we still couldn't stop overeating. The risk of diabetes, heart disease, high blood pressure, back problems, and joint damage aren't just theoretical bogeymen to us—many of us have suffered from them firsthand. Even before our physical health deteriorated, our quality of life suffered. The obsession with food governed our lives, while the fat immobilized us. Physical movement became a burden, and we suffered humiliation, ostracism, and discrimination because of our size.

Even those of us who were never obese suffered from terror at the thought that we would become fat because of our eating. Some of us purged, but even vomiting until we bled didn't make us stop.

We blamed ourselves. We blamed our parents. We blamed our bosses, our spouses, and our children. We blamed the government. We blamed the supermarkets. But finding a scapegoat never stopped us from stuffing our faces. We made resolutions on New Year's Day and broke them before nightfall.

We have tried to get in touch with our feelings. We have tried rolfing, religion, meditation, and self-actualization. We have tried every brand of psychobabble we could find. Some of us got great emotional benefits from our efforts at inner growth, but it didn't necessarily stop the growth of our waistlines.

Some of these methods may have brought relief to some. If they had worked for us, however, we would still be using them. We would never have come to OA.

Our members include those with eating disorders of the most chronic and severe kind, the kind that have resisted all other forms of treatment.

---

*Human chorionic gonadotropin (HCG) was a favorite of the shot doctors a few years ago.

One might think that with a disease as serious as ours that there is no hope, that we are doomed to overeat until the consequences kill us. Indeed, with people like us, who have failed at so many other treatment attempts, one might be amazed that *any* of us ever recover. And yet thousands of men and women in OA have recovered from the disease of compulsive overeating.

In OA we have found not a cure, but a solution. It's a way of life that ensures, one day at a time, that we don't kill ourselves with excess food.

℘ The basic approach

The premise of OA is that what works for other forms of substance abuse, such as alcoholism and other drug addiction, also works for compulsive overeating.

OA is modeled after Alcoholics Anonymous. AA was founded in the 1930s by two alcoholics who discovered they couldn't stay sober unless they worked with other alcoholics. Since then, millions of alcoholics have recovered through the AA program, and the same principles have helped countless others in related programs, such as Al-Anon (for the friends and family of alcoholics), Gamblers Anonymous, and Narcotics Anonymous. OA was founded in 1960 by Rozanne S., a Los Angeles housewife, after she accompanied a friend to a Gamblers Anonymous meeting and realized that what worked for gamblers and alcoholics could work for her.

OA meetings are set up much like AA meetings, and the same Steps and Traditions are followed. We have discovered that by changing the word *alcohol* to *food* we can identify very closely with the struggles of the alcoholic. Like AA, OA is a nonprofit organization that's supported totally by the voluntary contributions of its members.

OA approaches the problem of obesity from a different perspective than most weight-loss programs. Even though the majority of us came to OA to lose weight, we soon discovered that weight loss is not the end in itself, but rather a happy by-product of recovering from the compulsion to overeat. OA isn't a quick fix. Indeed, it's a slow fix, if you can call it a fix at all. Nowhere in the program are you promised a live-happily-ever-after cure. Unlike many commercial schemes, there is no pretense that you will learn to solve all your problems by going to a few lectures or by going on a diet with the group. What OA offers is a way of life that daily removes the craving for excess food. It's not an easy way of life; on the contrary, it requires a lot of time and effort. Probably few of us would have chosen it if we were not absolutely desperate to have our eating disorder lifted.

So what does this way of life involve? What goes on in OA meetings? Just exactly how do we get better? The best way to find out is to go to OA meetings—and that is just what I did.

My first meeting

This was the day. I was finally going to go to one of the meetings I heard mentioned on the answering machine. It started out like so many other days, with my finishing off a family-sized package of Reese's peanut butter cups. Lunch was a sandwich and some cookies that I picked up at the company cafeteria, and then there had been "Build Your Own Sundae Day" at work that afternoon. After work, I made a quick stop at the drugstore to pick up a one-pound bag of M&M's and a large Nestle's Crunch bar for dinner. As was typical of my eating in those days, I ate almost two pounds of straight junk food per day for my 240-pound body. Sedated by my fix, I headed for the OA meeting that would change my life.

I walked around the hospital looking for the meeting, apprehensive about what I would find. Would it be a bunch of five-hundred-pound freaks? Or would it be a bunch of size-obsessed people who had never been more than ten pounds overweight and who would babble on about what they did with their tofu and how many ounces they gained or lost last week? I couldn't find the meeting, so I asked at the information desk for directions. How embarrassing! (As if she couldn't tell by looking at me that I belonged there!) My heart was pounding as I approached the conference room, although I don't know if it was from nervousness or just the strain of all that walking.

I walked in. About thirty chairs were arranged in a circle, most of them filled. About two-thirds of the attendees were women, and only a few were noticeably overweight.

What are all these thin people doing here? I thought. It was obvious that this was another false hope, that these people knew nothing about what I was going through. It didn't occur to me until much later that the reason there were so many thin people there was that OA really worked. I looked around, expecting to see a scale somewhere. I didn't see one. There was, however, a table in the corner with a bunch of pamphlets on it. I waited.

A thin, attractive woman started the meeting by announcing that she was a compulsive overeater and then led the group in a short prayer known as the Serenity Prayer. *This is a waste of time,* I thought. *What does this woman know about compulsive overeating? And besides, what does this prayer have to do with being fat?*

Then she asked if there were any newcomers. I raised my hand and said that my name was Jim. Everyone in the room responded, "Hi Jim! Welcome!"

This is brainwashing, I said to myself. But then a little voice inside my head said maybe my brain could use a little washing. I still didn't think that this group would do me any good, and I resolved to go to the all-night supermarket on the way home from the meeting to pick up some more junk food.

After the introductions, someone read some things about how the program worked and how OA was run. Something about Steps and Traditions, which mostly went in one ear and out the other. Then the leader explained that she was going to share her experience, strength, and hope by telling what she used to be like, what happened, and what she was like now.

I was expecting some saccharine tale about how she had lost ten pounds through Jazzercise and lived happily ever after. Instead, she told a tale of addiction to food that left me amazed. It was a tale of diets and shot doctors, legal and illegal drugs, of pounds gained and lost and regained and lost and regained again. It was a tale told by someone who knew what it was like to be unable to stop eating. Someone who had been there. Someone who knew what it was like to eat until it hurt and to keep on eating. I heard her admit to doing things with food that I had done and would never even think of telling another human being, let alone a group of strangers. I discovered that I was not the only human being who had trouble finding clothes that fit; who had lied about food; who had left the house at 3:00 a.m. on a winter morning to go to the all-night grocery store; who often had a sticky steering wheel in the car; and who had left candy wrappers everywhere.

I discovered that I was not alone. I also discovered that there was hope, and that I didn't have to live that way anymore. I still didn't know how to go about changing the way I lived, but I was willing to follow directions. *Doing it my way had gotten me into this mess,* I thought. *Maybe if I did what these people suggested I might get what they had. I might even get below two hundred pounds.* The speaker announced a break and suggested that newcomers purchase literature at the literature table.

I waddled over to the table. A woman walked up to me and asked if I needed a sponsor. I didn't know what a sponsor was, so she explained: "A sponsor is another person in the program who works with you individually. They aren't your boss or therapist, and you can change sponsors at any time. You can have as many sponsors as you want and you don't pay them anything. Most people start by working out with their sponsor what they are going to eat each day. A sponsor is also there to lend a sympathetic ear and to pass on helpful suggestions."

She asked me if I was ready to start right then and there. I told her I was. She made sure that I picked up some literature as well as a meeting list and arranged for me to call her the next morning. She suggested that I try to make it to ninety OA meetings in ninety days.

I had nothing to lose except 110 pounds, so I thought I would give it a try. That night, I was able to skip going to the all-night supermarket. I started going to a lot of OA meetings and applying what I learned there to my daily life. Ten months later I was 110 pounds lighter, and I have been maintaining ever since.

This book is an attempt to pass on what has helped me so much. I hope it's as helpful to you as OA has been to me.

❦ Is OA for you?

A common question asked by curious people is, How do I know if OA is right for me? Only you can answer this question. OA will work for you if 1) you are a compulsive overeater and 2) you are desperate enough to devote time and energy to getting better. You probably know by now if you have a problem with food. To find out if your problem is severe enough so that you have the willingness to work the OA program, take a good look in the mirror and see if you are like us:

Do you find yourself eating more than you planned again and again? Have you tried and failed at other methods to control your eating or your weight? Have you repeatedly gained back weight you have lost? Have you used vomiting, laxatives, or compulsive exercise to avoid the consequences of your binges and found you could not stop doing so? Have you ever lied to yourself or others about how much or what kind of food you ate? Is your obesity or your eating behavior a threat to your health? Have you given up important social activities because of your overeating? Has your obesity or your eating behavior impaired your performance at work or your relationships at home? Do you spend a great deal of time thinking about food? Have you continued to overeat even when you knew that overeating was making you miserable? Have you ever tried to hide the amount of food that you were eating? Do you have a collection of diet books whose advice you meant to follow but didn't? Do you use the pretense of being a gourmet as an excuse for being fat?

If you have been nodding your head and saying, "Yes, that's me" to more than a few of these questions, I have bad news for you: You have a serious food problem. The good news is that there is hope. This book is a complete guide to the Overeaters Anonymous program, which has helped thousands of men and women recover from eating disorders just like yours.

How to begin

By now many of you are probably wondering, *How do I get started?* This section provides some nuts-and-bolts details on how to begin.

One thing to remember is that there is a tremendous amount of freedom in OA to work the program as much or as little as you want. There are no OA police who will bust you. Indeed, you will see people doing many different things. The test that you should apply is this: Is it working for them?

The first thing to do is to start going to OA meetings. You are free to attend as few or as many meetings as you like. There is no set requirement. But the more meetings you go to, the better off you will be, especially early in recovery. You may also quit at any time; there are no obligations. We often suggest that newcomers try at least six different OA meetings before they decide that the program as a whole isn't for them. We suggest this because the tremendous variety of available meetings will give newcomers more of a chance to find meetings that they like.

You can usually find meetings by looking up "Overeaters Anonymous" in the telephone book. If not, try calling the Alcoholics Anonymous number to see if they have any information on OA meetings in your area. Don't give up too easily; it may be difficult to find where meetings are being held in your area even if there are a lot of them. As a voluntary nonprofit association, OA doesn't often advertise. Once you get to a meeting, though, you can usually obtain a list of local meetings.

If you still can't find a meeting near you, try writing or calling the World Service Office of Overeaters Anonymous at P. O. Box 92870, Los Angeles, CA 90009. Don't worry—the literature they send you comes in a plain envelope with only a box number on it, so your mail carrier or family won't find out that you have sent for information from OA.

You will discover that meetings are held in all kinds of locations, from hospitals to libraries to banks to church basements. Since some locations may be hard to find, it's advisable to call ahead for directions.

Don't be worried about being the largest or smallest person at the meeting. You will find all shapes and sizes. Every age, race, creed, social class, sex, and sexual preference is represented in OA. But remember that a meeting will reflect the backgrounds of those who attend it. This means that a downtown lunchtime meeting will likely be attended by people who work in downtown offices, while a morning meeting in suburbia will have its share of suburban homemakers. In college towns, you will find a lot of college students. If you don't find what you need at one meeting, try other meetings until you do.

Of course, there is more to OA than just going to meetings. Much is in written form that you can read at your leisure. You can buy most of the conference-approved OA literature and some of the more popular AA books at many OA meetings. Usually, meetings provide some pamphlets free to newcomers, but you will have to pay for books. Since the literature person is a volunteer, and since it takes time to restock literature that has sold out, I recommend that you purchase books and pamphlets whenever you see them. If you delay, it may be a while before you get another chance.

For starters, I recommend stocking up on these pamphlets, all of which are published by OA.

- *A Program of Recovery*
- *To the Newcomer*
- *Questions & Answers*
- *The Tools of Recovery*
- *A Commitment to Abstinence*
- *Compulsive Overeating and the OA Recovery Program*
- *Before You Take That First Compulsive Bite, Remember . . .*

But there is even more to this program than you will hear at your first meeting or read in the pamphlets. Undoubtedly, you will have many questions. At most meetings, a notepad is circulated on which members write their first name and phone number. Feel free to copy down as many of the phone numbers as you wish so that you will be able to call other OA members later with your questions. They will be more than happy to answer.

Also, it's very helpful to find a sponsor. At many meetings, available sponsors are asked to identify themselves, or they may also indicate that they are available on the notepad. Just walk up to one of them after the meeting and ask them to help you get started. Another way to get a sponsor is to find someone who seems to have a good recovery from overeating, someone you can identify with, and ask him or her to help you. If the person you have asked to sponsor you declines, you could ask him or her to help you find someone who can. Arrange a convenient time to call, and let your sponsor do the rest.

I will say more about sponsorship later. For now, try to get a sponsor quickly. Don't get hung up in the trap of looking for the perfect sponsor; there is no such thing. I have had sponsors who were far from perfect, but they gave me what I needed.

☙ Go to meetings

Once you have decided that you are ready for OA, then you are ready to do what we do. Getting to as many OA meetings as you can in the early days will help you to get better faster. You will find people in every stage of the disease and in every stage of recovery. A lot of what is said may seem strange at first, but it will eventually start to make sense. Going to meetings does take time. No one who has lost weight in OA and kept it off will tell you that it doesn't. But when I put in the time and go to a lot of OA meetings, it becomes ridiculously easy to eat properly; when I don't put in the time, it gets harder to eat properly.

Take my word for it, going to as many OA meetings as you possibly can is the easiest, softest way. I have watched many people try to get well without going to a lot of meetings and they get nowhere fast. If one meeting a week could fix us, then our favorite commercial diet club might have cured us all a long time ago. Remember that we in OA are the hard-core cases that no other program could help. If our eating disorder were a simple problem to solve, we would have solved it by ourselves long ago without help from anyone.

❦ Read the literature

Along with the pamphlets previously mentioned, there are several books you will find very helpful. Although the order in which you read them is probably not too important, I recommend starting with *The Twelve Steps and Twelve Traditions of Overeaters Anonymous,* which describes how we apply the Twelve Steps of AA to compulsive overeating. I next recommend the book *Alcoholics Anonymous,* often called the "Big Book."* The Big Book is the basic text of AA that describes precisely how a bunch of drunks recovered from alcoholism.

We have found that the AA Big Book is a pretty good guide to recovering from overeating as well. Since OA is modeled after AA, just read the AA book and substitute the word *food* for *alcohol* and you will have a good idea of what OA is all about. Other useful books include *Overeaters Anonymous,* which contains inspirational stories about how others recovered in OA, and *Living Sober,* an AA book with useful suggestions for living one day at a time without drinking, which also works for not overeating. Eventually, you should also read the AA book *Twelve Steps and Twelve Traditions.*

Something to watch for: Not all the material on sale at meetings may be official OA literature. Some groups carry additional literature that they believe is helpful, although most groups feel it's best to stick to official OA publications. If you want to find out whether what you are reading officially reflects the thoughts of OA as a whole, look for the Conference Approved Seal on or near the back cover. This doesn't mean that you shouldn't read anything else, only that the material may not reflect the views of OA.

❦ Put the fork down

You will hear time and time again that OA isn't a diet club, but the fact remains that in order to recover you have to eat properly. Don't worry

---

*When the first edition of *Alcoholics Anonymous* was published, it was printed on thick paper because the founders wanted purchasers to think they were getting their money's worth. The first edition was an inch thicker than the current third edition, even though the third edition has an additional one hundred pages. Thus, the Big Book really was big.

about the perfect nutrition plan for now; you can always fine-tune your food plan later. The most important thing when you are getting started is to stop bingeing your brains out. This will help clear your mind of the fog that's induced by eating too much. Stop eating sugar and junk food and eat reasonable quantities of healthy food. If this seems impossible, it's not. Trust me. Go to a lot of OA meetings and find out from other overeaters how they did it.

Be prepared to go through physical withdrawal when you stop overeating. If you had felt wonderful the moment you stopped overeating, you would have stopped a long time ago. You may be so used to eating enormous quantities of the wrong kinds of food that your body will react when you start eating sanely. Withdrawal from overeating may not be as dramatic as coming down from heroin, but neither is it the most pleasant thing in the world. You may feel tired and irritable, and you may also get headaches. You can expect severe cravings at times, but remember that they will pass.

❧ Take it one day at a time

At first, it may seem overwhelming to stop overeating and go to lots of meetings. You may think, *I could never possibly do this for any length of time. After all, what am I going to eat on Thanksgiving or at Uncle Fred's party next month?* Relax. You don't have to worry about things that far in advance. All you have to do is worry about getting through the next twenty-four hours. One thing we stress heavily in OA is to take life one day at a time. You can put up with all kinds of aggravation for short periods of time that you couldn't stand forever, and that includes withdrawal. You don't have to solve all of your problems right now; you just deal with the most important ones as well as you can and leave the other ones until later. So remember, just for today be good to yourself by not abusing your body with too much food, or with junk, and do whatever you need to do to get better.

Sometimes you must take it just one hour or one minute at a time. Remember then that within a few hours it will be mealtime again and you are entitled to another tasty and wholesome meal. Although your disease may tell you that your arm will fall off if you don't eat right now, the reality is that no one ever died of starvation between lunch and dinner. You managed to live while waiting for stuff to bake, and you will survive if you don't eat until your next scheduled meal. Not only will you survive, but you will be glad you didn't binge.

Just as you don't have to "future-trip" or project about things that haven't happened yet, you don't have to dwell on the past or in old ways of thinking. For example, your overeating is now part of your history; you can't change it, but you don't have to repeat it.

Most of us recovering overeaters refer to our overeating in the past tense because we don't plan to do it again. For example, saying "I ate when I went to the dentist" is a simple factual description. Saying "I overeat when I go the dentist" indicates that we are still planning to overeat the next time we visit the dentist. Using the past tense is a good mental trick to help us think of overeating as no longer being a viable option.

The major insights of OA

This section discusses the four major insights that many of us have gotten from OA and how they reflect some of the thinking behind the program:

- The weight is only a symptom.
- A new lifestyle is necessary.
- Do for yourself what you see working for others.
- The principles of Alcoholics Anonymous also work for compulsive overeating.

❦ The weight is only a symptom

Our obesity was only a symptom of our eating disorder. Let's face it, we never would have gotten fat if we hadn't eaten more calories than we burned. Most of us fat people have lost weight many times only to gain it back. Many of us in OA have lost weight equal to several human beings during our many years on the yo-yo cycle. We always thought that if we just managed to lose the weight, we would live happily ever after and our weight problem would go away forever.

Unfortunately, that weight was never really lost. We always found it again. If we ever did hit our goal weight, it was only for a brief moment and then we started eating again and regaining our fat. As one OA wag put it, "We were experts at snatching defeat from the jaws of victory." There is just something about our bodies that makes us want to eat more food than we need, and no amount of dieting is going to fix that.

Thus, the real goal for us isn't to reach a number on a scale, but to eat sanely and rationally. In OA, this is known as abstaining from compulsive overeating. If we are eating the right amounts of wholesome food, our weight will eventually be exactly where it should be.

This is a pretty hard pill for us to swallow. It means that in order to lose the weight and keep it off, we have to quit overeating. We must get rid of the delusion that after a period of dieting we can go back to our old way of eating without going back to our old weight. I know that in my own case I wanted to have my cake, eat it too, and be thin at the same time!

So with our history of insane eating, how do we manage to eat sanely and rationally? Fortunately, we don't have to do it alone. We can learn from the experience of other insane eaters who have gone before us and recovered. But we must change not only the way we eat, but the way we live.

❦ A new lifestyle is necessary

The second major insight follows the first: Once we realize we have an eating disorder, we need a new lifestyle, because our old one has stopped working. We need to replace overeating with something better. Many of us once thought that if only we lost the weight, or if only we found the right magical diet, we could go merrily on our way. But we realized that if we continued to live the way we used to live, we would continue to eat the way we used to eat. And if we continued to eat the way we used to eat, we would continue to weigh what we used to weigh.

We attempted to use food as a weapon in domestic arguments, as a tranquilizer, as entertainment, as a study aid for school, and as a navigational aid while driving. We are experts at using any excuse to overeat. Whether we had a broken heart or a broken shoelace, it seemed to us that food would fix it. Whether we were glad, sad, mad, busy, or bored, we could turn any event into an excuse to eat. And we did. Despite the fact that food did a lousy job of doing the things we wanted it to do, we kept on using it.

When we finally put down the fork, we needed to find other ways of doing the things that we tried to do with food. If we try to stop overeating without trying to change the way that we deal with the rest of our lives, we are going to have a very difficult time indeed.

This new lifestyle affects not only what we eat, but also how we act, think, and feel. We learn ways of using our feelings as opportunities for growth rather than excuses to overeat. We clean up the wreckage from the past and put our lives together in a way that works without self-destructive overeating.

Life will provide you with just about every possible excuse to overeat. In the future, you will undoubtedly have problems with your family, your job, and your neighbors. Self-destructive eating won't fix any of those problems. Overeating won't put dollars in your bank account, turn your relatives into the people you want them to be, or win you a promotion at work. Overeating won't write your term papers or improve your exam scores. But this new way of living is strong enough to withstand all the shocks that life can throw at it.

A major problem with our past weight-loss schemes was that we could never stick to them. We would start off with a great deal of enthusiasm and meet with a lot of initial success. After a while, though, we would tire of them and allow ourselves to become distracted. The result was that we returned to overeating and regained lost weight.

How do we adopt this new lifestyle? How do we put our lives together so that we don't have to overeat and so that we don't forget our problem? Haven't we tried to develop new lifestyles many times before with exercise routines, therapy sessions, and New Year's resolutions? What is different this time? Now, through the OA fellowship, we have the experience of other people who have eaten the way we have and who have gotten better. We aren't doing it alone anymore. We have the support of other overeaters like us, and we have newcomers remind us of how serious our problem is. In OA, we learn from those who have what we want.

❦ *Do for yourself what you see working for others*

OA is a practical program based on the experience of thousands of overeaters over many years. We concentrate on learning from each other—doing for ourselves what we have seen working for other overeaters. There is very little theory in OA about how to cure eating disorders. The organization doesn't have any grand philosophy about what causes people to overeat. Most OA members aren't trained as doctors, neurobiologists, or therapists, although there are many in the fellowship. The purpose of OA isn't to analyze ourselves and figure out the reasons why we overate. As the saying goes, "If you want to find out why you overate, stop overeating."

If you ask ten OA members what causes eating disorders, you will get twelve different answers. They can't all be right. Some in OA say they are addicted to specific foods; others will talk about a spiritual malady. Some believe eating disorders stem from an oppressive patriarchal society or improper parental training. Dysfunctional families are often mentioned.

I believe that I have a genetic predisposition to overeating and that my body reacts differently to food than that of a normal person. When I feel like devouring the entire supermarket, it gives me some peace of mind to know that it's only my brain chemistry that's out of whack. I know that this too shall pass, and that I don't have to overeat because of it. It raises my self-esteem not to think of myself as stupid, childish, or emotionally damaged because I have an eating disorder.

The bottom line is that the causes of compulsive overeating are irrelevant for the purposes of getting better. This is mind-boggling to those of us who have spent years in therapy trying to figure out the root causes of our overeating. We always thought that if we figured out why we overate, we would magically learn how to control it. Yet somehow, despite the best therapists, we still couldn't. The image I like is that of a house on fire—I may know that the fire was started by a match, but blowing out the match won't put out the fire once the house has started to burn down. All we really need to know is that we overate because we are overeaters. I have heard it said at meetings that understanding is the booby prize, because it doesn't stop us from overeating.

Those who work the OA program recover, regardless of their beliefs about the origin of their eating disorder. I have had many debates with my OA friends about what causes overeating, and I have noticed that even people with views vastly different from my own manage to get better. My observation is that everyone who recovers takes the same actions. They may have a variety of beliefs about what caused their overeating, but they have some things in common: they go to a lot of OA meetings, read the literature, talk to other overeaters on the phone, and use all the tools and Steps.

Many of us thought that we were totally different from everyone else, but it was only the twisted thinking of our eating disorder. For example, we thought the rules that applied to everyone else, simple rules like "If you eat too much, you will get fat," didn't apply to us. We thought that no one knew what our problem was like and that no one could possibly understand. In OA, we call this state "terminal uniqueness."

The truth is that our disease made us feel that way. Although we overeaters are different from "normal" people, we have many things in common with other overeaters. There are people who understand. We don't have to struggle alone with our problems anymore. We can learn from the experience of those who have gone before us.

My standard advice to newcomers is this: Don't take my word about what works. Take your own survey. Go to a lot of different OA meetings and find the people who have been where you are and who have what you want. Then find out how many meetings they attended, how they ate, what they read, what actions they took to get better, and what they do now to stay better. But for now, don't get hung up on *why* they do those things; you will be able to figure that out later. As is often said in meetings, "More will be revealed."

The fellowship of OA is a tremendous information resource for anyone interested in eating disorders. There are meetings in all fifty states and dozens of foreign countries. When you put all of us together, you have literally millions of years of combined experience with the disease and the recovery from it. There is a lot of information out there to be harvested by anyone willing to search for it.

I can't overemphasize the importance of this information network. Remember that the founders of AA discovered they could stay sober only when they worked with other alcoholics. It's much the same with OA; it's not a program that you can work alone in your kitchen. By getting to know the other people in the fellowship, you can learn from their experiences. You don't have to keep reinventing the wheel all by yourself. You can follow the paths that others have blazed before you.

Somewhere in OA there is someone who has been where you are. I have met all types of people in OA from all walks of life, including a bulimic doctor who weighed 320 pounds. I have met several people who have lost more weight than I have ever weighed. There are people in OA who have been through every type of weight-loss method or eating disorder program—from Weight Watchers to psychiatric hospitals to intestinal bypass surgery. There are lawyers, architects, and Harvard MBAs, as well as steelworkers, housewives, and students. I am continually amazed that when I share a problem at meetings, I discover other people who have had the same problem. I can learn then what they found useful in dealing with the problem.

Much of this knowledge is communicated by example, both good and bad. When we get to know people and see how they deal with crises in their lives without overeating, we gain strength from their example. But when we see people return to overeating, we remember the pain that overeating caused us and become much more grateful for the benefits we have accrued since we quit overeating. We also learn from the mistakes of others so that we don't have to repeat them.

As was pointed out to me long ago by an OA old-timer, "You don't have to understand this program, you don't have to believe it, you don't even have to like it. All you have to do is do it. And it works."

❦ The principles of Alcoholics Anonymous also work for compulsive overeating

Compulsive overeating is a disease that's similar to alcoholism. Applying the principles of the extremely successful Alcoholics Anonymous program allows us to recover from compulsive overeating.

Alcoholics Anonymous was founded in 1935 by two alcoholics who discovered that they couldn't stay sober by themselves. Individually, they had tried for years to stop drinking but couldn't do it. They knew that just one drink would set them off on a drinking bout, but knowing this didn't stop them from picking up that first drink. They each had tried joining a religious group, but that didn't do it either. It was not until they began to work with other alcoholics that they were able to achieve long-term sobriety. Since then, AA has helped millions of alcoholics around the world achieve lasting sobriety. The early AA members synthesized the philosophy and method of their recovery program into the Twelve Steps and Twelve Traditions, which have been copied and adapted by all of the other Anonymous programs. That's why Anonymous programs are sometimes referred to as Twelve Step programs. I discuss the Steps further in part 2, but for now I offer a short summary of their principles for overeaters:

1. *Admit to yourself that you have a problem.* You can't do anything about your overeating if you can't admit that it's a problem.

2. *Rely on a Power greater than yourself.* The Anonymous programs aren't religious organizations and don't compete with any churches, but they have found some spiritual concepts quite useful. Belief in a Power greater than ourselves is one of them.

3. *Clean up the wreckage of the past.* Most of us have a lot of problems that we have to face up to as a result of our overeating. We need to take a good hard look at ourselves, figure out where the problems are, and move on. We need to patch up our relationships and adopt a new way of living that keeps us from wanting to overeat.

4. *Work intensively with other compulsive overeaters.* By helping other overeaters to achieve what we have, we remind ourselves of the nature of our disease and of one of the things we have to do to get better. We help other overeaters by attending OA meetings, talking to each other on the phone between meetings, and by working with each other on a one-to-one basis.

More about compulsive overeating

OA doesn't know what causes people to overeat. It is a pragmatic program of recovery that focuses on the solution rather than the problem. Although OA doesn't seek to reveal the various causes of overeating, we in the program have, nevertheless, learned quite a bit about compulsive overeating from our own experience. This section discusses several ways of looking at compulsive overeating in OA, all of which are useful in different ways. We don't pretend to know all the answers, and we realize that there is much to be learned.

❦ *Compulsive overeating is a disease*

Webster's Ninth New Collegiate Dictionary defines *disease* as "a condition of the living animal or plant body or of one of its parts that impairs the performance of a vital function." I think most of us are willing to agree that the consequences of our overeating severely impaired our functioning. We are all aware of the medical consequences of severe obesity, and many of us have suffered from them. Indeed, almost every overeater has heard the infamous lecture from the well-meaning doctor: "If you don't lose weight, you'll suffer from high blood pressure, heart disease, joint problems, back trouble, . . ." Many of us had already started to suffer from at least one of these problems.

We have also had our emotional functioning impaired by our overeating. There was the mental craziness of our obsession with food and weight, as well as the sense of failure we felt after each unsuccessful weight-loss attempt. Not only did we dump on ourselves, but we have also suffered from the ostracism imposed on us by our fat-phobic society. The stares, the names, the rude remarks, and the difficulty in finding employment added burdensome emotional weight to our already overwhelming physical weight.

Some of us cringe at the word *disease.* It sounds like something that might be contagious. Many of us have quibbled in OA meetings over such fine points, preferring to call our problem by another name. Some of us prefer to think of our disease as "dis-ease."

The semantics are irrelevant. It doesn't matter whether we call compulsive overeating a disease, a problem, an eating disorder, or a whatchamacallit. The fact remains that it's a very serious condition that has caused us all a lot of pain and suffering.

But what exactly is the disease of compulsive overeating? How can it be treated? I learned in OA that compulsive overeating is an eating disorder that's cunning, baffling, and powerful. It's an illness that affects its victims physically, emotionally, and spiritually. Beyond this vague description, there is no official OA-approved cause or definition. OA leaves these questions to the scientific community and instead concerns itself with helping victims recover. As one overeater put it, "It doesn't really matter whether I have bad genes or whether I hate my parents. What matters is that I have an eating disorder that can ruin my life. I have to deal with it, since there is no cure yet."

One thing that we do know is that we can stop blaming others for our overeating. We have to take responsibility for our own recovery. The bottom line is that we picked up the food and put it into our mouths. Nobody tied us down and forced us to eat.

❧ Compulsive overeating is not a moral issue

By viewing compulsive overeating as a disease, we get away from faultfinding and get on with our recovery. One of the great lessons I have learned in OA is that compulsive overeating is not a moral issue. So many of us have been told that we are "good" if we are dieting and "bad" if we aren't. It was a relief to learn that I was not a bad person because I was fat. We aren't bad people who need to get good, but sick people who need to get well. None of us woke up one day and decided, *I am going to overeat compulsively and pursue self-destruction to the gates of insanity and death.* It just happened.

We really don't know what causes eating disorders, but one thing we do know is that they aren't voluntary. No one would volunteer to handle problems by going out and gaining a hundred pounds or vomiting five times a day. Nevertheless, that's how we have handled problems, and that's part of our disease.

One thing I have noticed is that people with eating disorders aren't stupid. We are intelligent and have accomplished many things in our lives. But when we were practicing our food addiction, our brains were fogged by it. Just try to eat a pound of chocolate in ten minutes and see how clearly you can think afterwards. I know many highly educated people in OA, including doctors, lawyers, therapists, MBAs, and Ph.D.s.[*]

Nevertheless, a lot of the popular explanations for eating disorders assume that the victim is so stupid that he or she overeats for some trivial reason. Some theories blame the victim of the eating disorder by asserting that we think overeating will solve our problems. We aren't bad people who need to be saved and we aren't stupid people who need to get smart. To repeat: We are very sick people who need to recover.

I get upset when I hear oversimplistic generalizations like "Fat people are afraid of people and need to build a wall of fat to keep them away." If I wanted to keep people away, I could find better ways of doing it than eating myself into morbid obesity. For example, I could stop taking baths.

❦ Compulsive overeating is an addiction

For reasons that aren't well understood, overeaters continue to eat to excess despite repeated attempts to control their eating. Like the alcoholic, the overeater is baffled by the insane behavior of returning to self-destructive eating. We have all seen it time and time again, and we have experienced it personally. Many of us have lost weight only to regain it. The yo-yo syndrome is no joke if you are the yo-yo. *Why did I eat so much? Why can't I stop eating? What is wrong with me?* These are questions we have asked ourselves many times over, and yet never really found a satisfactory answer.

The parallels between compulsive overeating and other forms of substance abuse are striking. In the *Diagnostic and Statistical Manual for Mental Disorders,* Third Edition Revised (DSM-III-R), the American Psychiatric Association lists the currently accepted definitions of most mental disorders.[†] The diagnostic criteria for psychoactive substance dependence are listed in the left-hand column. I've responded to each criterion in the right-hand column. In order to be diagnosed as dependent, one must meet only three of the criteria.

---

[*]OA surveys its membership every couple of years. One striking result of a recent survey was that OA members are better educated than most Americans. As one doctor friend put it, "We got straight A's in school, but managed to flunk life."

[†]*Diagnostic and Statistical Manual for Mental Disorders,* 3d ed., revised (DSM-III-R) (Washington, D.C.: American Psychiatric Association, 1987), 167.

Diagnostic criteria for psychoactive substance abuse

My experience

1. Substance often taken in larger amounts or over a longer period than the person intended.

I sure ate more than I planned on many occasions.

2. Persistent desire or one or more unsuccessful efforts to cut down or control substance use.

I wanted to lose weight and tried to diet many times without success.

3. A great deal of time spent in activities necessary to get the substance (e.g., theft), take the substance (e.g., chain-smoking), or recover from its effects.

At times I went hours out of my way to get the food I wanted and spent hours baking large quantities that only I would eat.

4. Frequent intoxication or withdrawal symptoms when expected to fulfill major role obligations at work, school, or home (e.g., doesn't go to work because hung over, goes to school or work "high," intoxicated while taking care of his or her children), or when substance use is physically hazardous (e.g., drives while intoxicated).

Food doesn't produce the extreme intoxication of other drugs, just a persistent mental fog.

It was certainly unsafe to drive while wolfing down food.

5. Important social, occupational, or recreational activities given up or reduced because of substance use.

Oftentimes I avoided being with people because I wanted to eat, and my obesity kept me from doing many things I wanted to do.

6. Continued substance use despite knowledge of having a persistent or recurrent social, psychological, or physical problem that's exacerbated by the use of the substance (e.g., keeps using heroin despite family arguments about it, tolerates cocaine-induced depression, or has an ulcer made worse by drinking).

Despite my rising blood pressure, chest pains, shortness of breath, and trouble finding work, I still couldn't stop overeating.

Diagnostic criteria for psychoactive substance abuse	*My experience*
7. Marked tolerance: need for markedly increased amounts of the substance (i.e., at least a 50 percent increase) in order to achieve intoxication or desired effect, or markedly diminished effect with continued use of the same amount.	My standard binges went from eight-ounce bags of M&M's to twelve-ounce bags, to one-pound bags, to a one-pound bag plus a candy bar.
8. Characteristic withdrawal symptoms.	I felt cranky, irritable, tired, and had severe cravings.
9. Substance often taken to relieve or avoid withdrawal symptoms.	I certainly ate to feel better when I was cranky, irritable, or tired.
10. Some symptoms of the disturbance have persisted for at least one month, or have occurred repeatedly for a longer period of time.	It lasted all of my life until I came to OA.

Does this sound familiar? We may respond addictively to just some foods or to food in general. Just as the alcoholic is never satisfied with just one drink, the compulsive overeater is never satisfied with just one bite.

Normal people can be satisfied with just one cookie or one piece of cake, but not me. Even if it were possible for me to have just one without devouring the entire batch, I would still crave more. The only time I could stop after I started eating that stuff was when I ran out or when it just plain hurt too much to shove more into me.

My major binge food was plain M&M's, although I could abuse anything. There was about a year during my adolescence when I didn't eat any chocolate because of my acne, but I ate a lot of other sugary junk food.

I don't remember how I started overeating again. One day I was just eating the stuff, despite the fact that my acne was still there and the dermatologist told me not to eat chocolate. I knew that the stuff was making me fatter and messing up my face and probably shortening my life, but I did it anyway. Despite the fact that I knew how harmful chocolate was to me, I would enter what the Big Book calls "those strange mental blank spots" when I was without defense against that first bite.[*]

[*] *Alcoholics Anonymous* [the Big Book] (New York: AA World Services, Inc., 1976), 42.

That's how most of my diets ended. There usually was no traumatic crisis to produce a binge. Often, there wasn't even a binge, just some innocuous occasion when it seemed perfectly natural to make an exception to my diet. Once the diet was broken, it seemed perfectly natural to return to my usual eating habits, which meant overeating. Before I knew it, I had regained all my weight and was wondering what had happened.

As with most addictions, mine was progressive, and my quantities kept increasing. At first, the vending-machine-sized bags of M&M's were enough to satisfy me. But eventually those would disappear in one gulp, so I moved on to the larger bags. The eight-ounce bag would last me a while, but then that wasn't enough; I wanted more immediately after devouring one. I moved on to the twelve-ounce bags. Finally, I was snarfing the pound bags in only a few minutes, and then would have a big Nestle's Crunch bar for dessert. A few hours later, I would want more.

Like other addicts, I hid my behavior because I didn't want others to see how much I ate. Although they must have known from my forty-six-inch waist that I was eating a lot, I almost never did my real eating in front of others. They just didn't know what it was like to really *need* food the way I did.

I would sneak food into my room so that my family wouldn't see me eat. Disposing of the wrappers was a problem, since they would tend to pile up. Fortunately, M&M's wrappers are rather flat, so I could hide them behind books or in my desk. I was still discovering hidden wrappers two years after I stopped eating M&M's.

I would go to different stores on different days so that the clerks wouldn't see how much I was eating. Often, I would eat in my car, leaving a sticky steering wheel and a mess of candy wrappers and crumbs.

I knew that the stuff controlled me and that it was killing me. I knew that I was an addict and that I had to stop. So I did, on my own. For me, giving up junk food was like Mark Twain's alleged remark about quitting smoking: it was easy; I'd done it hundreds of times. But sooner or later I would pick up that first bite and get right back into the food, although during my "dry" periods my tolerance for massive quantities of junk food lessened. When I started eating it again, I discovered that the eight-ounce bag of M&M's would appease my craving, which had been previously sated only by an entire pound.

My addict's brain thought I was cured! I thought that I could now eat my drug in moderation and live happily ever after. Little did I realize that the food had taken over one more time and that I would again need ever-increasing quantities. Before I knew it, I was back to the one-pound bags.

I don't know why chocolate has such a powerful effect on me. Perhaps it's the theobromine or caffeine, the fat in the cocoa butter, or just the massive amount of refined sugar. Perhaps it has something to do with the way I was fed as a child. I don't really know why. I just know that I am addicted to it. The first bite sets off a desire for more and more. If I don't take the first bite, I don't have to worry about the second or the hundredth.

When I stopped eating my binge foods, I went through withdrawal, another characteristic feature of addiction. I felt cranky, tired, and irritable. At times, the cravings were intense. Some people experience severe headaches; others report nightmares. But the symptoms do pass. With the support of OA, I was able to make it through.

Chocolate isn't the only food to which I am addicted. Anything with sugar in it—and that includes honey, fructose, and corn syrup—sets off a craving for more. I don't pretend to know why this is. It may be some inborn genetic defect or chemical imbalance in my body, or perhaps it is the result of years of consuming it to excess. All I know is that I couldn't stop eating it on my own and that I feel much better without it.

There is another whole category of foods to which my body is overly sensitive, but perhaps not addicted. Some people refer to this as a food allergy, but I don't like to use the term. To me, *allergy* means that I will break out in hives or something dramatic. What happens instead is that the cravings for more food seem stronger when certain foods are in my diet. Virtually anything very starchy seems to make me want more food, so I feel better off leaving such things as bread and potatoes out of my food plan.

I don't pretend that everyone shares my food sensitivities, nor does OA. Some of us went crazy on dairy products (which haven't presented a problem to me). Salty foods have done in others. Fats and oils are a problem category for some. Most of us can binge on anything, although certain foods seem more dangerous than others.

❦ *Compulsive overeating isn't a single condition*

It's clear that compulsive overeating isn't a single uniform problem with a single common denominator. It doesn't take long to see that compulsive overeaters come in many different shapes and sizes, and with many different histories. Some of us, like me, overate and had been fat all of our lives; others started overeating in adolescence or later. Some of us gained the weight in extremely rapid binges; others gained it a few pounds at a time over many years. Some of us store fat in our midriffs; others in our hips. Some are also alcohol and drug abusers; others aren't. Some are chocolate junkies; others couldn't care less about chocolate.

The mysteries of the human appetite are still poorly understood. Many biological factors are involved, including the size, number, and type of our fat cells, as well as the way our body regulates the glucose in our blood and the serotonin in our brain. A great deal of evidence from adoption studies indicates that a tendency toward obesity is inherited from one's biological parents, even if the children are raised by others.

Even though modern scientific evidence suggests that there really is something different about the bodies of compulsive overeaters—that it's not just all in our heads—many social and cultural factors are also involved in eating behavior. Genetics alone can't explain why many Americans eat turkey on Thanksgiving.

I won't get into the "nature versus nurture" arguments about human behavior. Both heredity and environment appear to be involved in ways that are extremely difficult to disentangle, even for the most skilled researchers. As overeaters, we can change neither our heredity nor our past environment. We must learn to live with the consequences of what life has handed to us.

The point is, it's highly likely that a variety of causes result in compulsive overeating. Thus, we compulsive overeaters aren't all alike. A fever can be the sign of many different diseases, so all fevers should not be treated the same way. Likewise with overeating.

This diversity has a major implication. This means that there is no one-size-fits-all OA food plan. For years, OA published food plans that served as effective weight-loss diets. There were great debates within the fellowship about what should be included in these food plans. Over the years, however, OA recognized the diversity of needs within the fellowship. Not everyone has the same physical sensitivities. Not everyone in OA needs to shed pounds. Thus, for a variety of reasons that I will discuss in detail later, OA stopped publishing food plans in 1986.

But despite the amazing diversity within our fellowship, and despite our disagreements on what to eat, we agree on a surprising number of things. We especially agree that applying the principles of Alcoholics Anonymous to compulsive overeating lifts the compulsion to overeat.

❦ A cure hasn't yet been found for compulsive overeating

We have all tried many things to end our overeating. If any of them had cured us, we wouldn't need OA. The medical profession has tried to relieve our pain and suffering. Unfortunately, they haven't been too successful with weight loss. Countless diets and nutrition plans have been devised over the years, some of them by the most experienced experts in nutrition. But no matter how good or balanced the plan, we overeaters just couldn't stick to it. Medically supervised fasts are effective at shedding a large number of pounds quickly, but when we went back to our old way of eating, we gained all of the weight back and then some.

Many drugs have been tested to help overeaters, such as thyroid hormones, amphetamines, and antidepressants. None of them has yet proved safe and effective for long-term weight control. The way I see it, any drug treatment would have to be powerful enough to alter brain chemistry, yet safe enough to take for a lifetime. Maybe someday they will find a cure, but I can't afford to hold my breath waiting for one. What I need is a way of life that will get me through today without overeating.

A wide variety of surgical treatments have been tried, and many of them, such as intestinal bypasses, have been abandoned as a result of major complications. The techniques that are still being tried, such as stomach stapling, do not remove the compulsion to overeat; they just make the overeating more painful. I met one stomach-stapling recipient who claimed to have burst a staple during a binge; I've met others whose overeating was so severe that they managed to gain weight even after the surgery.

Numerous skilled therapists have developed treatments for overeating—from Freudian analysis to hypnosis to behavior modification. And we have used nearly every brand of therapy. These treatments may have worked for some, but for many of us any success was as short-lived as our diets—we gained the weight back.

Let me make one thing clear: Even though the medical and psychological communities haven't cured our eating disorders, we hold nothing against them for it, because we know that they have sincerely tried and are still trying to help us. It's not their fault; it's the baffling nature of the disease. They provide enormous benefits to us in other areas. Maybe someday they will find a cure for overeating.

Since no cure has yet been found for our problem, what we need is a form of treatment that will allow us to live as complete and as full a life as possible. We need a way of life that will last for the long haul, that will get us through everything that life can throw at us.

If a person's kidneys stop functioning, toxic wastes build up in the blood and kill the person. Dialysis artificially cleanses the blood so that the person can live. Essentially, the blood is taken out of the patient, filtered, and returned without the waste. It's imperfect, and expensive, but it does work. It's not a cure; the patient usually has to undergo treatment for the rest of his or her life. In much the same way, OA isn't a cure but a "spiritual dialysis" that cleanses us of the toxic food thoughts that would otherwise build up and kill us.

What OA isn't

There is a lot more to OA than meets the eye. It takes time to comprehend the program fully in all its aspects. As I think about this, I am reminded of the old tale about a group of blind people who each feel one part of an elephant and think they know what an elephant looks like. The one who feels a leg thinks that an elephant is a tall animal shaped like a tree. The one who feels the trunk thinks that it's a snakelike animal that flies through the air. One who feels the tail thinks that an elephant is an animal that closely resembles a hanging vine. Since it's easy to get a distorted view of the OA program from only a meeting or two, this chapter removes a few common misconceptions.

❦ OA isn't a diet club

Dropouts or graduates from other diet clubs, such as Weight Watchers and TOPS, may get the impression that OA is just another club designed to help members lose weight. After all, many of us came into OA because our fat was making us miserable. But dieting isn't the purpose of OA. Indeed, the word "diet" itself is almost never used. Most of us were veteran dieters when we came into the program. I had been on and (mostly) off diets continuously since the age of ten. I can count the calories on a plate of food from fifty feet and balance food groups with my eyes closed. But none of that helped me to stop eating compulsively. Indeed, if my dieting had worked, I wouldn't have needed OA.

Most of us know from our own sad experience that fad diets are not maintenance diets. A diet, in the popular sense of the word, is merely a *temporary* change in our eating patterns designed to remove excess fat without dealing with our underlying eating disorder. Remember, the weight is merely a *symptom* of overeating. If we go back to our old way of eating, we will soon be back to our old weight. What we need is a way of living without excess food.

This isn't to say that food can be ignored. Indeed, virtually every successful OA member makes sure that his or her body gets the proper nutrition. Nor does it mean being obsessed with the calorie count of every food. Rather, it means being aware of the body's true needs and meeting them appropriately. Our disease has a strong physical component—the mechanics of how our bodies react to food—and any overeater who ignores the physical side is in grave danger of returning to compulsive overeating. The OA program gives us a proven method for relieving the craving for excess food, but it's not going to turn us into people who can eat whatever we want whenever we want. To quote *Alcoholics Anonymous:* "We are like men who have lost their legs; they never grow new ones."[*] I don't believe that I will ever be satisfied by one piece of candy. No matter how long I abstain from overeating, I will always be an overeater.

That's why the OA program puts so much emphasis on abstaining

---

[*] *Alcoholics Anonymous*, 30.

from compulsive overeating rather than on dieting and weight loss. What we strive for is a wholesome, nutritious way of eating that we can live with for a long time. If our food is clean—if we are eating the appropriate amounts of nutritious food—then the weight will take care of itself. As long as I don't overeat, I have a chance at recovery.

❧ OA isn't group therapy

From the outside, OA may look like group therapy: a place where members sit in a circle and discuss their problems. Even though there may be a superficial resemblance, OA meetings are run in a different way. For one thing, there is no professional moderator. After all, in an organization with no dues or fees, who could pay a professional's fee? Instead, each meeting is led by a member, and most meetings rotate leaders periodically. In place of a costly professional or an elected leader, each group is governed democratically by consensus, which we call *group conscience*.

Another major difference is the way in which the discussions are held. In some group therapy settings, participants are sometimes encouraged to confront each other. In OA, the opposite is true. Back-and-forth conversation—called *crosstalk*—is strongly discouraged. Members usually get the opportunity to speak once, although they are certainly not required to say anything. They are free to share whatever they need to share without having to worry that someone will cross-examine or argue with them. Sometimes there is a topic for discussion and sometimes there isn't. The discussion at times may appear to have very little to do with food.

The basic purpose of meetings isn't to discover why we ate or to dump our emotional garbage. Some people think that the purpose of a meeting is to talk about problems so we won't eat over them, but that's not quite true either. The purpose of a meeting is to share with each other what works and what doesn't for recovering from our eating disorder. Random dumping of life's woes doesn't accomplish that. Our job is to "carry the message, not the mess." Merely complaining about our problems isn't the point; discussing how we deal with them without overeating is.

❧ OA isn't a religious organization

Some people think that just because we start a meeting with a prayer we must be a bunch of religious kooks. Or they think that we are going to try to change their personal religious beliefs. We certainly don't want to change anyone's religion; in fact, we encourage members to practice the religion of their choice. OA isn't a religious organization, it's a pragmatic one. We have found many spiritual concepts very useful in our recovery, so we use them.

Recall that the only requirement for membership is a desire to stop eating compulsively. That's it. Nothing else. We mean that. Really. You don't have to believe in a god or in prayer in order to join. If the talk about a Power greater than yourself bothers you, you can do what many have done and use the OA group as their Higher Power. Membership doesn't require a belief in any god that you don't want to believe in. Members don't have to believe in any particular creed in order to belong, and the program does not conflict with any major religion. Indeed, the principles of the AA and OA programs have been endorsed by leaders of all major religions and denominations.

Nevertheless, most meetings start and end with simple prayers like the Serenity Prayer. The spiritual side of the program has helped most of us accept that we have an eating disorder and that we can learn to live with it. If the spiritual side is anathema to you, just remember to take what you need and leave the rest. If you are worried that your friends might think you've joined a cult, remember that no one has to know about your OA attendance. OA members range from devout atheists who wouldn't be caught dead in a church, to born-agains, and everything in between. OA represents all segments of society.

❦ *OA isn't a cult*

Some newcomers are afraid that OA is a cult. They hear discussions about spirituality at the same time they hear that OA isn't a religion and get confused. They observe that newcomers are treated with a large amount of attention and encouraged to spend a lot of time going to meetings. They wonder if OA could be some kind of front for the Moonies.

I can assure you that OA isn't a cult. There is no guru who seeks to control your life, nor any dogma to which you must swear allegiance. OA takes no position on outside issues, so you won't be told how to vote or which church to attend. There are no dues or fees, so you won't be asked to turn your life savings over to the cause. Nor will you be asked to solicit contributions on street corners or pass out literature in airports.

You don't have to believe anything to be a member of OA—you need only the desire to stop eating compulsively. Everything we recommend is only a suggestion. It's up to you to take what you need and leave the rest.

❦ *OA isn't easy*

OA doesn't promise a miracle cure. It takes a lot of effort and a lot of time to recover from an eating disorder. If you think that there is an easier way, go and try it. If it works for you, great! If it doesn't work, OA will still be there.

When I say that OA isn't easy, I mean two things. First, OA requires a willingness to thoroughly overhaul the way we live. Most of us were not willing to do that until we were defeated by food. Second, it requires a big investment of our time. We spend hours going to meetings, making phone calls to other OA members, and reading the literature. I have found that when I spend the time, it becomes easy for me to eat properly. When I don't put in the time and don't get to meetings, the all-night supermarket starts to call to me again.

Remember that for most of us, OA was the last house on the block. If there were an easier and softer way to recover from eating disorders, we would be doing it.

☙ OA isn't professional

OA isn't a group of professionals; it doesn't support itself financially by charging overeaters for weight-loss services. In other words, OA isn't a group of trained dieticians, therapists, or spiritual directors. The strength and success of OA come from the personal experience of all OA members. OA can usually help a suffering overeater when other methods have failed.

Many well-meaning people have tried to help us over the years with a variety of suggestions, diets, therapies, and exercise programs. We have felt alone because these helpful people, no matter how sincere their desire to help, didn't understand our problem. They didn't understand the compulsion and the cravings, the need to eat the way we did. When I was new in OA, I met a lot people who had eaten like me and who had been obese like me and who had recovered. To me, they had a lot more credibility than any title or diploma could bestow.

However, we aren't trying to compete with anyone, nor do we wish to. OA can serve as a helpful supplement to virtually any type of weight-loss or eating-control program. I have known many who participated in other commercial weight-loss programs and got additional support in OA. Hospitals with eating disorder units have found that their patients do much better with OA participation.

OA doesn't claim to be the only way to get well. But we are particularly good at reaching overeaters who have been unreachable by other methods.

Recovering from an eating disorder can be tricky medically, especially if a person has other medical problems. We urge members to get competent professional advice.

We also don't compete with professional therapists. Many problems are best handled by competent therapists. Indeed, it seems that most members of OA could benefit from professional therapy at some point in their recovery.

How effective is it?

The OA program may sound good in theory, but does it really work? OA has worked for me; it has taken 110 pounds off my body and kept it off since 1982. I have met OA members who have maintained their goal weight for decades.

Measuring the effectiveness of OA is a difficult task. Because of the anonymous nature of the program, we don't keep records on anyone. No one is ever required to give their full name or to weigh in. We don't even have a list of our full names. Even if we did have such a list, it would be difficult to measure exactly what each individual was doing. We don't keep meeting attendance records; thus we don't know who is really attempting to follow the program and who is just a spectator.

Nevertheless, my own belief, based on over ten years of going to meetings, is that it does work *if you work it.* That means going to OA meetings frequently, reading the OA and AA literature, talking to other overeaters on the phone, and making a good-faith effort at abstaining from overeating and working the Twelve Steps.

In 1986, the OA World Service Office conducted a survey of OA members by sending out questionnaires to a sample of meetings. Of those responding to the survey, 75 percent had lost between ten and one hundred pounds, 3 percent had lost more than one hundred pounds, and 22 percent had either gained weight or weighed the same as when they started, although this 22 percent included 9 percent with less than one month in OA. Thus, if we correct for the newcomers, 85 percent of those who stuck around OA for more than a month lost weight.*

That's a miracle. OA was a last resort for most of us. Collectively, we have tried and failed at just about every other weight-loss scheme. That it works for *any* of us hopeless types would be a major accomplishment; that it works for so many of us is an outright miracle.

I must point out, however, that not everyone who walks through the doors of OA immediately loses all excess weight and keeps it off forever. For some people, it takes a while before enough of the program sinks in to have an effect. Some attain a great deal of emotional growth without yet attaining their goal weight; others relapse and temporarily regain part or all of their weight. But even those who relapse rarely gain all of their weight back, and they usually lose it again after a period of struggle. My observation is that everyone who sticks around OA benefits substantially. In other words, everyone who keeps coming back usually loses weight as well as grows emotionally. Furthermore, OA gives us the opportunity to have a complete recovery—one that involves our physical, emotional, and spiritual well-being.

---

*For more information, see the OA publications *Survey Report* and *Survey Highlights.*

Many of us have had the experience of losing weight and still feeling crazy. Or we learned to pretend that we loved ourselves while we were killing ourselves with food. Being a normal person, I not only want to feel good about myself, I want a healthy body. OA gives me the opportunity to have that kind of complete recovery.

❦ Who benefits from OA?

In discussing effectiveness, we must ask, For whom is it effective? Since everyone in OA isn't the same, it's likely that OA works better for some people than others. What follows may be particularly useful to those who are wondering whether they should recommend OA to a friend, relative, or patient.

The severely obese. OA works particularly well for those who suffer from severe long-term obesity, especially those who have tried and failed at many other weight-loss schemes. In OA, they will find a fellowship of people who know what it's like to be obese and can help them.

Bulimics. OA also works well for bulimics. Those who have binged and purged—whether by vomiting, taking laxatives, starving, or exercising compulsively—can also find relief in OA, even if they have never been obese. (Not all bulimics are thin, however. I have met many extremely obese people who purged and still managed to stay very fat.)

Addicts who are also overeaters. A number of recovering alcoholics and drug addicts find their way into OA. After getting sober in AA, they discovered that they had switched addictions—to food. "Hot Fudge Sobriety" finally brought them to OA to overcome their compulsive overeating.

❦ Who doesn't benefit from OA?

It's also valuable to know who doesn't get much out of OA so that people don't waste their time in the wrong place. As a group that focuses on helping compulsive overeaters, OA can't be all things to all people. But I don't want to scare anyone away. If you think that you can benefit from OA, try several different meetings. If you like it, great. If not, the only thing you've lost is a few hours of your time.

Those not suffering from eating disorders. Common sense says that if you don't have an eating disorder, you won't get much out of OA. Occasionally, someone without a serious eating disorder will wander in and want to stay because of the camaraderie, support, and fellowship. They may be lonely or wish to work on emotional development, but OA won't do much for them if they don't have an eating disorder.

Some who try OA suffer more from perfectionism than an eating disorder. Not everyone who is overweight by ten pounds has an eating disorder. And not everyone who has ever barfed is a bulimic. A normal person can stop such self-destructive behavior; compulsive overeaters, on the other hand, can't stop by themselves.

Lightweights. Can we talk? There is a national hysteria going on about weight loss. We all know that those who are more than thirty or forty pounds overweight run an increased risk of disease and early death, and that walking around with a hundred extra pounds is like being a human time bomb. However, the risks associated with ten or twenty extra pounds (for otherwise healthy people) are small and still open to debate.

Today, fashion says to be thin. A hundred years ago, fat was in. This obsession with thinness may be more destructive than the excess weight. Grade-school children are now becoming obsessed with diets and many are developing bulimia.

It's more dangerous to yo-yo than to carry a stable ten or twenty extra pounds on your body. Each time you starve yourself, you lose muscle. When you gain the weight back, you gain fat instead of muscle. Even if you end up at the same weight at which you started, it's likely that the percentage of fat in your body will be higher than before.

My observation is that those who only want to lose a few pounds for cosmetic reasons don't stick around OA very long. They are usually not desperate enough to be willing to make the complete life overhaul. Since they aren't desperate enough to work the complete OA program, they usually don't have a lot of success and eventually leave in frustration. The people who stick around and succeed in OA are the ones who know that their health is on the line. OA won't do much for those who want to lose three pounds to look good in a bathing suit.

Young children. Unfortunately, OA hasn't had much success with young children. As one who has suffered the agony of growing up fat in a fat-phobic society, it's painful to see that OA doesn't yet have an effective means of reaching preteens. It would be wonderful to spare these kids the pain of growing up as an overeater. I have seen many people start meetings for young people in several different parts of the country, but few of them have flourished.

Once kids reach their later teens, the situation improves. By that time they are usually mature enough to accept their problem and work the OA program. I have met many overeaters who began their recovery when they were teenagers. The young people with the greatest success have been those who regularly participated in OA meetings, although it can be difficult for a young person without transportation to get to enough meetings to recover.

Pure anorexics. Anorexia nervosa is a serious and often fatal eating disorder in which the victim starves himself or (usually) herself. In the classic anorexic (the "restrictor"), the victim doesn't overeat at all, but continually undereats, often going to great lengths to conceal the fact. Anorexics have a distorted body image, seeing themselves as obese even when they are emaciated.

Many of us in OA have flip-flopped between over- and undereating. I have met several recovering anorexics/overeaters who gained over a hundred pounds coming out of anorexia. Such people can find help in OA. Others have suffered from the binge/starve syndrome, often resulting in emaciation. Such people can also find help in OA. But for the pure anorexic with no overeating problem (which is fairly rare), OA is the wrong place. For someone on the brink of death from starvation, hearing a bunch of people say "Don't eat no matter what!" could be lethal.

Many in OA are afraid to say that. We tend to be people-pleasers, afraid of rejection, so we tell everyone to keep coming back, even if they don't belong in OA. I suspect that pure anorexics would be better served by having their own Anonymous program, even though they are officially welcome in OA.

The founders of Alcoholics Anonymous knew that they had developed a very powerful set of principles that could solve a lot more ills than just alcoholism. But they also knew they had to focus on staying sober and helping other alcoholics achieve and maintain sobriety. That's why the founders of AA encouraged those with other problems to start their own fellowships, such as Narcotics Anonymous, Gamblers Anonymous, and Overeaters Anonymous. Likewise, the strength of the OA fellowship comes from the shared experience that all overeaters can use to help each other; we know what it's like to live with our disease. If we mix too many people in OA with dissimilar problems, that sense of fellowship will disappear.

Closed-minded know-it-alls. One thing OA stresses is to keep an open mind. We strive to work a pragmatic program in which we do what we see working for other overeaters. When we entered OA, many of us had to let go of our cherished preconceptions about what we had to do to get our weight off and keep it off. As someone pointed out to me soon after I got into OA, doing it my way had failed, so maybe I should try doing what worked in OA. My observation is that those who think they already know all the answers about eating disorders take longer to get well than those who keep an open mind.

❧ The dangers of OA

In all fairness, I believe some dangers are inherent in the OA program. Like any strong medicine, there can be side effects. For example, you will hear many people talking freely and sometimes graphically about how they have abused food. Some of these methods of abusing food may not have occurred to you before and you may be tempted to try them. In this way, OA could accelerate the progression of an eating disorder.

Believe it or not, some people find "binge buddies" in OA. Such people return to unhappy habits and attempt to drag their OA acquaintances down with them.

Some people fear that they may overdose on OA and become addicted to going to meetings. They fear that they may switch one compulsion for another. Even if this did happen, it would be a case of switching from a very self-destructive compulsion to one that's much healthier. But the beautiful thing about the program is that it is by nature a systematic means of breaking compulsive behavior. Becoming compulsive about OA just means that the compulsion will be lifted sooner.

But the biggest danger, in my opinion, isn't an overdose but an underdose of OA—when a person comes into OA and doesn't invest the time and effort needed to get well. He or she attends meetings sporadically and doesn't take the time to read the literature or talk to other recovering overeaters. Needless to say, such a person will keep having trouble with food and may end up quite demoralized.

Once you become aware of your food problem, it's difficult to go back to denying it. OA ruins your overeating. You realize that a binge is no longer a way to be "good" to yourself but a very self-destructive act.

The tools of recovery

By now you have learned how to get started in OA. You have an idea about the nature of the program, but it's likely that you also have questions. This section may answer some of those questions.

OA has a lot of slogans, most of which are shamelessly stolen from AA. Sometimes these slogans seem rather trite and simplistic, but they come in handy on many occasions. One of them is "Keep it simple." I have often heard it said that OA is a simple program for complicated people—we sometimes tend to complicate things by cluttering up the basics of recovery with extraneous details.

In an attempt to keep it simple, we in OA have distilled most of the fundamental actions that we take to get better into eight tools of recovery, which are discussed in the OA pamphlet of the same name.

The tools are often discussed at the beginning of OA meetings. Sometimes they are read out of an OA pamphlet; other times volunteers are called on to discuss the tools in their own words. There is good reason for this emphasis: virtually every single person with the type of recovery that I want uses all of the tools on a regular basis. In other words, the people who have lost the weight, who are keeping it off, and who aren't going crazy are the people who use all the suggested tools:

- abstinence
- sponsorship
- meetings
- phone calls
- literature
- service
- anonymity
- writing

This next section explains my own interpretation of these tools. One implication of keeping it simple is that when the unnecessary items have been removed, what is left is absolutely essential. Thus, we need to work all the tools in order to continue to recover from our eating disorder. Each tool has its own special use, its own time when it comes in handy. You can't maintain your home with only a hammer; you also need other tools like screwdrivers, saws, wrenches, and pliers. Moreover, you need to know where they are when you need them and keep them sharp and rust-free. You also need a certain amount of practice so that you know which tools to use, and when.

Likewise, you can't maintain your recovery with only one tool, such as only following a food plan. Furthermore, it's better to practice using the tools often, even if you don't feel like overeating, so you know how to use them when you do. To return to the home-repair analogy, the time to patch your roof is on a nice day, not in the middle of a thunderstorm.

❦ Abstinence

The first tool deals with food. The question of what to eat and what not to eat is very important to most overeaters. We have spent most of our life obsessed with food and diets and have lived with the painful consequences of our overeating. We all know instinctively that dealing with the physical side of our disease is extremely important. In OA we do this through something we call abstinence. Fortunately, abstinence doesn't mean what I first thought it did.

Abstinence means abstaining from compulsive overeating. It's both a goal of the program as well as a means to an end. Most of us in the program have discovered that we were so disabled by our eating disorder that there could be little physical, emotional, or spiritual recovery until we stopped drugging our bodies with excess food. Bingeing our brains out is a good description of the way we used to behave; excess food warped our brains as well as our bodies. Our addiction caused us to think in crazy ways that led to insane behavior. Why else would we have eaten so much when we knew that the food was killing us?

Fortunately, much of the craziness subsides when we get our binge foods out of our systems. The cravings also subside and a certain amount of clarity enters into our thinking. When I was bingeing, I knew that I *needed* my binge foods. Now I know that my survival demands that I live without them.

But the transition from serious bingeing to contented abstinence is rarely quick or easy. Your body goes through a withdrawal period when the physical and emotional cravings for excess food are still there. Fortunately these pass and your brain clears up so that you can think clearly. Also, the weight starts to come off, which is really great.

The benefits of abstaining from overeating are tremendous. First, a great feeling of self-esteem comes from the fact that we are no longer abusing our bodies with excess food. We can think clearly and begin to deal with our problems rather than smother them in food. As we abstain from overeating, the discipline we develop about food extends to other areas of our lives and we become more productive at work and more attentive to our families. As one OA member put it, "When my food is crisp and clean, my life is crisp and clean. When my food is fuzzy, my whole life gets fuzzy."

By now you are probably wondering, So what do I actually eat? Remember that the diversity of the OA fellowship precludes a one-size-fits-all food plan. But I will describe more about the specifics of what worked for me later on.

In OA, each person is the judge of his or her own abstinence. Since each person is different and has different nutritional needs, as well as different food sensitivities, no particular food plan is right for everyone. Nor will the same food plan be right for the same person at different times. The important thing is to be honest with ourselves about what and how much we are eating. After all, if we eat too much or if we eat the wrong foods, we will suffer. A good question to ask ourselves is, Am I headed toward overeating or away from overeating?

At meetings, you will hear people define their abstinence in many different ways:

- "I eat three moderate meals a day with nothing in between but coffee, tea, and diet soda."
- "Abstinence means not eating my binge foods."
- "Abstinence is eating properly."
- "Abstinence is three weighed and measured meals committed to a sponsor."
- "Abstinence for me is almost a state of mind in which I just don't overeat because I don't want to overeat."
- "Abstinence is rational eating. It takes rational thinking to get to rational eating."
- "Abstinence is three meals a day and life in between."
- "Abstinence means eating in accordance with whatever food disciplines are appropriate for me."

- "Abstinence is the ultimate in pampering my body. It means not eating too much food and not eating too little. It means not abusing my body with junk food or food that makes me crazy. It's not the 'death-camp diet,' but an act of self-love."

As you can see, each person's idea of abstinence is different. For me, the foundation of my abstinence is not eating junk food and not eating between my planned meals. I know from personal experience and from observing other compulsive overeaters like me that I can't control my intake of certain foods, mainly foods loaded with refined sugar and flour. I also know that I really don't know the meaning of full or hungry, so I don't trust myself to be able to snack spontaneously. I know that if I start making exceptions here and there, before I know it I'll be eating nonstop once again. Beyond that, I know that I still have the ability to eat more "abstinent" food than I need, so I have to pay attention to the quantity I eat. This means somehow measuring my food most of the time. I don't walk around with a tablespoon around my neck to measure my food everywhere I go, but I take care to eat just the amount I need.

❦ Sponsorship

Sponsorship comes in many forms. This tool is the embodiment of one of the main principles of the program: By helping each other we help ourselves.

A sponsor is another compulsive overeater who agrees to help you in your recovery from compulsive overeating. A sponsor isn't a boss, shrink, nutritionist, or doctor. It's not the task of a sponsor to tell you what to wear or who to vote for. A sponsor, though, can be a tremendous source of information, advice, strength, and encouragement. The person being sponsored is known as a sponsee.[*]

Some people get sponsors to help them with various aspects of their program, such as a food sponsor to help in their choice of an eating plan, or a Step sponsor to guide them through the Twelve Steps. I don't believe in splitting up the sponsoring job like that; I believe the task of a sponsor is one of helping another overeater work the entire OA program.

But what exactly does a sponsor do? It varies, depending on the style of the sponsor and the needs of the sponsee. Typically, newcomers want to start off by dealing with the food, so they arrange to call their sponsor each day to discuss what they will eat.

Planning the day's menu with a sponsor is a great way to get rid of a

---

[*]A variety of terms are used to describe a person being sponsored. "Sponsee" and "sponsoree" are the most common. Sometimes cute names like "baby" or "pigeon" are used, but I don't like these terms because they are degrading.

lot of the craziness in the way we select food. Once we have decided what we are going to eat and tell it to another person, it becomes easier to stick to it. For example, when I have planned my food and discussed it with my sponsor, I know that I may have to defrost it before dinner, or that I have to purchase something on the way home from work. This makes it less likely that I will arrive home from work only to discover that my entire dinner is still frozen solid, thus tempting me to buy junk food at the store across the street. Also, the worst time for me to plan a meal is just before the meal, when I am usually hungry, tired, and in a hurry to eat. If the meal has already been planned, it's a relatively simple matter of preparing it. If not, I often get confused and find myself standing at the refrigerator door, unable to decide whether I want to eat the leftover chicken because it might spoil, or the beef because I think it might taste better . . . or whether I should go out to eat because I'm really too tired or lazy to cook tonight . . . or whether I should have yogurt because I am in a hurry . . . or whether I am getting enough calcium and fiber in my food plan . . .

Listening to another overeater planning his or her food is also helpful for sponsors because they get to observe what works and doesn't work for other overeaters. The process of developing a workable food plan takes much practice and experimentation. By listening to how other overeaters plan what they eat, we get a better idea of how to plan our own meals.

Different sponsoring styles. There are as many different ways of sponsoring people as there are sponsors. Some sponsors discuss food daily; others don't discuss it at all as long as the sponsee isn't having any problems. Some OA members talk with their sponsor on a daily basis; others check in less frequently. My sponsors over the years have worked in different ways, and I believe no one way of sponsoring is right for everyone 100 percent of the time. To take advantage of the many different sponsoring styles, an OA member is free to have as many sponsors as he or she wishes and to change sponsors at any time.

But how does one get a sponsor? I am reminded of the old saying, "When the student is ready, the teacher appears." At most meetings, available sponsors are asked to identify themselves. Those who identify themselves are looking for someone to sponsor. Some people may be able to sponsor but may choose not to advertise this at meetings. Feel free to talk to any or all of them. You may want to get their phone number and chat a few times before asking them to sponsor you. Ask them how long they have been in OA, and what their experience has been. See how they respond to your questions about how OA works. Then, if they still look promising, ask if they would be willing to sponsor you.

It really helps to have a sponsor who has had overeating experiences similar to your own and who has the kind of recovery you want. As I've heard said at OA meetings, "If you want to speak French, find someone who speaks French. If you want to lose weight and keep it off, find someone who has lost weight and kept it off." It also helps to choose a same-sex sponsor. This reduces sexual tension, and, besides, one can often identify better with a member of the same sex.

Don't worry about finding the perfect sponsor. There is no such animal. Some sponsors are right at some times but not at others. Sometimes we need a sponsor who will listen; other times we need a sponsor who will guide us. Remember that you can change sponsors anytime you want. There will be times when you have learned all that you can from one sponsor and it will be time to move on to another.

You need not worry about being a bother to your sponsor, either. Your sponsor gets more out of sponsoring you than you get out of being sponsored. That's something I found difficult to believe when I first heard it, but now that I have sponsored people I know it's true. Working with other overeaters is really the foundation of our recovery. When we work closely with others, we learn a lot more about how the disease of compulsive overeating works.

Often, it's easy for me to forget where I've come from; sometimes I think that since I have been maintaining a 110-pound weight loss for several years, I have it made and will never have to worry again. But when I work with other overeaters, I am constantly reminded that there is no known cure for my eating disorder, and that all I get is a daily reprieve.

When you watch others succeed, they show you how to work a successful program. When they make mistakes, they show you what to avoid. Also, the satisfaction and happiness that come from participating in another overeater's recovery isn't something you want to miss. After maintaining your goal weight for years, it's easy to get jaded and forget what it was like to purchase clothes in a "big and tall" or "plus sizes" store. But when your sponsee is euphoric because it's the first time that he or she has bought clothes in a normal clothing store in over ten years, part of that euphoria wears off on you and makes you very grateful for recovery.

What does it take to be a sponsor? The basic requirement is a commitment to your own recovery from compulsive overeating. But before you can share something you must have something to share, so a little experience in OA is important. At least twenty-one days of current abstinence is the usual minimum qualification; completing the written self-examination as part of Step Four is also recommended before you start Step sponsoring. Once you feel you are ready to sponsor, feel free to stand up at meetings and identify yourself as a sponsor. It's helpful to volunteer to help a newcomer get started. A newcomer is often too shy or afraid to ask for a sponsor, just as I was at first. I feel my life was saved when my first sponsor walked up to me and volunteered to help me get started. I don't think that this happens often enough in OA.

Sponsorship is such a large and rewarding part of OA that I have a devoted a full section to it later.

❦ Meetings

The people who are successful in OA are the people who attend OA meetings frequently. I don't know the number of meetings that you may need; we're all different. But if you are having trouble with food or are just plain feeling irritable, you should probably go to more OA meetings. As one OA friend of mine put it, "My doctor suggested that I go to a lot of OA meetings and repeat as often as needed."

Meetings provide us with a sense of belonging and fellowship that many of us previously lacked. To realize that we aren't alone with our eating disorder is comforting. We learn to interact with other people and practice the human relations skills that we never developed because we spent so much time alone with food. Meetings can also be enriching, since our stories are filled with the variety of human experience.

Meetings come in many different forms. Some meetings have just a discussion with no leader; other meetings have both a leader and a separate speaker. Some meetings study the OA and AA literature instead of having a speaker; other meetings focus on the special concerns of various groups, such as women or gays, or those who have been a hundred pounds overweight. I have even been to meetings for those who eat in a particular way. Even if a meeting has a special focus, OA traditions require that all meetings be open to anyone who wants to stop eating compulsively.

Hospital conference rooms, church basements, libraries, and other public meeting places (usually ones with cheap rent) are good locations for OA meetings. However, they can also be found in some unexpected places. I have been to regular OA meetings on the beach in Santa Monica, California, and even one in the conference room of a McDonald's restaurant!

A typical meeting format. Early arrivals often help to set up the chairs. At small meetings, chairs are usually arranged in a circle to facilitate sharing; at larger meetings, chairs are often set up theater-style. I have been at some meetings where members continually argue about the best way to set up the chairs. At OA meetings you will find people in all stages of disease and recovery, and some have a little further to go than others!

Meeting formats will vary according to the group and part of the country. But most meetings usually begin with the leader introducing him- or herself as a compulsive overeater and then leading the group in the Serenity Prayer:

God grant me the serenity
To accept the things I cannot change,
The courage to change the things I can,
And the wisdom to know the difference.

The OA program of recovery is then briefly explained, often by way of the Twelve Steps and Twelve Traditions of OA. The tools of recovery are also sometimes read and discussed.

Then leaders "qualify" by telling their own story of what it was like to be a compulsive overeater, what happened over the years, how they recovered in the program, and what they are like today. Leaders are just regular OA members and aren't paid for leading. Meetings usually have a different leader each week; it's the task of the program chair to arrange for someone to lead each meeting.

After the leader qualifies, a basket is passed to help defray the cost of rent, printing meeting lists, maintaining a telephone answering service, and other miscellaneous items. It bears repeating that contributions are entirely voluntary and there are no fixed dues or fees. Nobody keeps track of how much or how little you contribute, and no one will throw you out for not contributing. Considering the thousands of dollars we have spent on excess food, exercise programs, and pill doctors, OA is truly a bargain.

After a few routine announcements, available sponsors are asked to identify themselves, and then there is a break. During the break, people get up, walk around, and chat with each other. Coffee and other low-calorie beverages may be available.

After the break, there is usually a discussion. Before speaking, members often identify themselves by giving their first name only and stating that they are compulsive overeaters: "My name is Jim and I am a compulsive overeater." This identification isn't required, and many people identify themselves in different ways. Some people refer to themselves as recovering overeaters, others as food addicts or bulimics.

The items discussed at meetings vary significantly, and, as mentioned earlier, sometimes appear at first to have little to do with food. The discussions are usually orderly; crosstalk, interruptions, and direct questions are frowned upon. Giving advice is considered extremely bad form. This guarantees that each person who speaks doesn't have to face the embarrassing prospect of immediate comment from another member. This also makes it easy for people to talk about whatever they need to, even if it concerns a sensitive subject.

You will notice that there is little talk about specific foods at OA meetings. One thing we have learned over the years is that merely recounting our last binge doesn't do us much good. We already know what food tastes like and we already know how to overeat. Merely describing past binges doesn't stop us from repeating them. In OA, we prefer to keep the focus on how we can restructure our life so that we no longer binge.

At some meetings, it's considered bad form to mention specific foods. The rule of thumb is to mention foods only when it's pertinent, and even then, don't dwell on the details. No one needs to hear an in-depth description of a Dove Bar. The world is already saturated with tantalizing food advertising.

Some people in OA feel that if we were really recovered we wouldn't be bothered by hearing about specific foods. That may be true, but we aren't perfect, and some of us may be quite shaky at any given time. There are times when hearing binges described in detail may be upsetting and spark the desire to overeat. Thus, we owe it to each other to avoid excessively detailed stories of food exploits that may start a fellow member drooling.

At the end of the meeting members join hands in a circle, and those who wish to may recite a prayer, which is often left up to the speaker. After a meeting people go out for coffee and continue talking. This "coffee therapy" can be the best part of a meeting, and I highly recommend it to anyone with the time to spare.

☙ *What if there aren't many meetings?*

I have been fortunate enough to live in cities with strong OA programs. Not everyone is so lucky. In many parts of the country and the world, there are few OA meetings. Or there may be few people with long-term recovery to learn from. Don't despair. Many things can still be done to make up for the lack of good meetings. Here are a few suggestions:

- Listen to cassette tapes of meetings.
- Read the literature.
- Go to OA conventions.
- Go on OA retreats.
- Contact other overeaters through the mail.
- Start your own meeting.
- Pick up the phone.

Listen to cassette tapes of meetings. The OA World Service Office in Los Angeles can send you order forms for tapes of OA conventions and meetings. Many OA groups maintain a library of these tapes that members can check out. Listening to them can be inspirational, and they are good to listen to while driving.

Read the literature. There is a lot of good literature about recovering from an eating disorder. Read it. *Lifeline,* OA's monthly magazine, is often called "a meeting in your mailbox." It also provides a listing of upcoming OA conventions and retreats.

Go to OA conventions. OA conventions are a fantastic way to meet other recovering compulsive overeaters from all parts of the globe. An OA convention consists of meetings, workshops, plays, and dances. It usually lasts for two or three days. The World Convention is held in a different city each year. Regional conventions are also held at various times throughout the year. Conventions are a good place to find the people who have been where you have been and who have what you want. Get their addresses and then start writing to them.

Go on OA retreats. Retreats are smaller than conventions and are usually led by one person who shares his or her program in depth during the retreat weekend. The quality of retreats varies significantly, but you can usually meet people who are very serious about their program.

Contact other overeaters through the mail. If there aren't enough meetings in your neighborhood, keeping in touch with other recovering overeaters through the mail is a good way to strengthen your program. You can find people to write to by going to OA conventions and retreats, or by writing to the World Service Office. They have a sponsor-by-mail program to help you get started.

Start your own meeting. If there aren't enough OA meetings near you, start one of your own. This is how OA has spread around the world.

☘ Phone calls

The telephone also provides a lifeline for those dangerous moments when the cravings hit. This can happen at almost any time, and often for no apparent reason. People without food compulsions usually can't understand what food cravings are like, but people in OA do, and they can lend a sympathetic ear when the food starts calling. It's amazing how just admitting to another human being, "I feel like overeating," helps make the feeling go away. Sometimes the people you call will have helpful suggestions; other times they will listen sympathetically. Some of the people you call will have so many troubles that yours look trivial in comparison. And, of course, on some days you will get lots of busy signals and answering machines. Nevertheless, the telephone can provide instant access to other compulsive overeaters who know what it's like and who are willing to help. I have telephone numbers that I can call any time of the day or night. Can you call your Weight Watchers lecturer at midnight when the "Aren't you hungry?" ad on TV has gotten your juices flowing?

But don't wait until the craving hits before you pick up the phone. Successful OA members make a habit of regularly talking to other people in OA. They get used to talking to others *before* they need it, so that when they do need it, using the phone becomes a reflex action. By making regular phone calls to other OA members, you find out who is home and when they can talk. You also find out who you best communicate with.

What does one say on an OA call? Of course, there is no set formula. Often, program people don't even mention food when they talk to each other; they just share a little bit about what is happening in their lives. Usually, I call up just to say hi. I will often talk about the minor dramas of daily life, such as parking tickets, job stuff, and goings on in the neighborhood. Sometimes, I call up a newcomer and ask if he or she has any questions about the program; other times, I call people with specific questions, hoping they can give me useful feedback.

Telephone calls are cheap. Even long-distance calls are cheaper than food.

☘ *Literature*

It helps to make a regular habit of reading the literature, such as the pamphlets sold at the meetings, the AA Big Book, and the daily meditation books, such as *For Today.* Not only does reading teach us more about how to work the program, it teaches us more about how to live life. Reading OA and AA literature can also help reinforce us during those moments of temptation when the food calls.

I want to put in another pitch for the book *Alcoholics Anonymous.* Although written as the basic text for AA more than fifty years ago, its lessons are extremely useful to overeaters. It's true that you have to wade through sometimes archaic and sexist language, and you have to keep substituting *food* for *alcohol,* but the results are worth it. Every overeater with the kind of recovery that I want has made a thorough study of the Big Book.

Another AA book on the must-read list is *Twelve Steps and Twelve Traditions,* which describes each of the Steps and Traditions of AA in detail. It was written over a decade after the Big Book and demonstrates a more long-term view of the Steps. *The Twelve Steps and Twelve Traditions of Overeaters Anonymous,* written specifically for OA, is a relevant and useful guide to applying the Steps to compulsive overeating.

OA also puts out a collection of books and pamphlets. *Overeaters Anonymous,* sometimes called the "Brown Book" because of its brown cover, contains a set of inspirational stories of people who have recovered in OA from compulsive overeating. However, it doesn't have a nuts-and-bolts discussion of how you actually go about recovering in OA.

I highly recommend subscribing to *Lifeline,* OA's monthly magazine, which contains stories of recovery contributed by individual OA members. As with meetings, sometimes it's great and sometimes it's not so great, but it's usually worth reading. To preserve your anonymity, it comes in a plain envelope with only a box number on it.[*]

---

[*]Other literature that many overeaters find useful includes *Living Sober, Alcoholics Anonymous Comes of Age, As Bill Sees It, Came to Believe,* and *Pass It On,* all published by Alcoholics Anonymous. Books that provide some background on the philosophy that motivated the AA founders include *The Varieties of Religious Experience* by William James and *The Sermon on the Mount* by Emmet Fox.

❦ Service

The slogan "You can't keep it without giving it away" is heard often in the program. Broadly defined, service means doing anything to carry the message about OA to another compulsive overeater.

A lot of work goes into a successful OA meeting, and not all of it's apparent when you walk in. Someone had to arrange for the meeting space. Someone had to set up the chairs. Another person arranged for the speaker. The coffee didn't miraculously appear from nowhere; someone had to make it. Literature had to be written, edited, printed, stocked, shipped, and set up for sale at the meeting. Another person had to count the money and make sure that the rent and literature got paid for. The meeting schedules didn't type themselves, nor did printers print them for free. Telephones didn't answer themselves; someone had to do that. Others had to arrange for meeting notices in newspapers.

Some service is impromptu, such as helping to set up chairs or cleaning up after a meeting; other service involves long-term responsibility, such as being the meeting treasurer. The longer-term responsibilities are usually divided up at business meetings (sometimes called steering committees), which are special meetings that follow the regular meetings, usually once a month.

Why do service? It's often said that the weight comes off faster if you do service. My observation of others in the program has led me to believe this. Those who do service seem to learn the program faster and thus find it easier to abstain from compulsive overeating. Almost every person with long-term recovery from compulsive overeating does service. By holding a job at a meeting, we are more likely to attend meetings regularly and thus receive the benefits of frequent attendance. Also, it forces us to get to know overeaters in the program and gives us a chance to work with others, which is the foundation of our recovery. It helps us feel included. Finally, service gives us something to do in our free time and keeps our minds off the refrigerator and the all-night grocery stores. If you don't believe me, try it.

❦ Anonymity

Anonymity means many things in the program. At its most basic level, it assures that the privacy of the individual is respected. No one need ever know that you are a member of OA. When we first came in, many of us were embarrassed at the thought of telling others about our membership. I thought things like, *What if it doesn't work? I'll look like a fool! I don't want people to know that I'm a compulsive overeater!* Of course, with my forty-six-inch waist, anyone could tell by looking at me that I had an eating disorder. Many of us, especially bulimics, aren't noticeably obese, and we may be reticent about announcing our problem to people who may not understand. That's okay. It's up to each individual to decide if, when, and to whom to reveal OA membership.

Last names and titles are rarely used in OA. This helps us realize that we are all compulsive overeaters in this program, and that no one is any better than anyone else. Eating disorders don't respect social position. However, it's not forbidden to use last names within meetings, and it's often useful to know someone's last name. For example, if you lose an OA friend's phone number, it's easier to look it up in the phone book than hope to bump into him or her at a meeting.

Anonymity also means that gossip is kept to a minimum. It's a breach of confidentiality to pass on any information about an OA member, even information shared at a large meeting, if that person would object. This makes it possible for trust to develop within the program and for members to share deeply personal matters without fearing that their secrets will be broadcast throughout the town.

Anonymity keeps us humble. Excessive pride is a common character defect in many of us, and anonymity helps us to remember that we are compulsive overeaters who are all just one bite away from a binge.

❦ Writing

We write to take a good hard look at ourselves and to find where our problems are. Writing is an essential part of the personal inventory we take in Step Four. Some OA members write daily. Even if we don't write daily, it's useful to write regularly about our problems and other things that upset us, because it will help us to stay out of the refrigerator. It's also a valuable tool for venting extreme emotions that we may be tempted to take out on our friends and families. The insight and clarity gained by writing down our thoughts and feelings are well worth the time it takes.

But you don't have to become an author to recover in OA. Your writing doesn't have to be poetic or even coherent. No one need see it except you. The important thing is that you use your writing to focus your thinking. After you have written something, you may wish to read it again to see if additional thoughts and feelings surface. Perhaps there is something you wish to pray about or meditate on. Discussing your writing with another person may also be helpful. Some overeaters who write about resentment or troublesome personal problems burn their writings as a symbol of getting beyond their problems. Burning it is also a practical means of making sure that the writing doesn't fall into the wrong hands.

Potential objections to OA

By this time, you might have several objections to OA. Perhaps you're ready to chuck it out the window. Please read this section before you decide that OA isn't for you.

You may be worried about the time spent in OA activities. Yes, it does take a lot of time, but if you have suffered from food the way we have, it's time well spent. Rather than spending my waking hours fighting the painful cravings for food or drooping in sugared-out lethargy, I now have energy and vitality and can enjoy life. I can be productive at my job and present for my family. I feel good about myself and have a sense of serenity that I never dreamed possible. I almost forgot to mention that I also have a lean healthy body.

I don't pretend, however, that the time is worth it for everyone. You must decide for yourself. If you haven't suffered from food very much, you may decide that OA isn't worth your time. Personally, if I could eat whatever I wanted to, have no ill health effects, and never be more than thirty pounds overweight without OA, I would do it. You owe it to yourself to investigate the program by trying several different meetings. Not everyone who walks through the doors of a meeting stays. That's fine. We will still be here if you do decide to try OA later.

If you think that you can find a better way, please try it. If it works, congratulations! As a matter of fact, if you find a better way, please tell me about it. But before you tell me, be sure to build up some credibility first. I only want to hear from someone who has lost over a hundred pounds and kept it off for five years. I don't want to hear some theory from someone who has never been fat, or about some approach that hasn't yet stood the test of time. The beautiful thing about OA is that it has passed the test of time that so many other weight-loss methods fail.

You may object to specific parts of the OA program, such as the prayer used at the end of meetings. Don't let your objections to one part of the program deny you from benefiting from the rest of it. Try to live with the parts that you don't like the way you live with commercials during your favorite TV shows; you may not like the commercials, but the show is still worth watching.

Maybe you feel that some other part of the program is impossible. For example, you may think that you will never be able to do some of the things suggested in the Twelve Steps. Many of us have felt exactly the same way. Don't let such attitudes block you from getting what you can from OA; talk to other OA members and find out how they handled those parts of the program.

Perhaps you have been to a few meetings and remain unimpressed by what you've seen. Don't give up so easily. You owe it to yourself to try several different meetings, since OA meetings vary widely. Also, make sure that you explore the OA and AA literature so that you have a good idea about what is going on.

Or perhaps you feel that you can't possibly keep up such a program for a number of years. Relax. We only have to take life one day at a time; we don't have to worry about what we are going to do two years from now. And remember, you can leave whenever you want.

II
Working the Program

Only by being willing to give up the safety of the old
can I find out what the new has for me.
Uncertainty, confusion, and fear of leaving the safety of the old ways
behind me are natural, but the need to save my life pushes me on.
I move beyond my fears and prejudices and learn
that I don't have to act on them; that, one day at a time,
I can face whatever must be faced.
—*For Today*

What should you eat?

This part of the book goes into more detail about how to work the OA program to recover physically, emotionally, and spiritually. I start with physical recovery, and then move on to the emotional and spiritual parts. I chose this order because newcomers often ask questions about the physical part first. This isn't to say that one part of recovery is more important than another. There will be trouble if any part of the recovery process—physical, emotional, or spiritual—is neglected.

One thing I have learned is that as long as I am eating sanely, what I eat becomes a less important part of the program. I have also noticed that those who work the rest of the program—by going to meetings, working with a sponsor, and reading the literature—get the food part of the program together sooner or later.

Although compulsive overeating has much in common with alcoholism, there is one major difference: the alcoholic can live quite well without alcohol, but the overeater has to eat in order to live. Many of us have gone back and forth between bingeing and starving. Sometimes it would seem easier not to eat at all. One story often told at meetings compares the addiction to a dragon. The alcoholic can lock up the dragon and throw away the key, but the overeater has to walk the dragon three times a day when he or she eats. Imagine trying to recover from alcoholism if your life depended on getting three—and only three—drinks a day, or if you had to worry about whether you could drink wine but not vodka!

Here is another analogy. Alcoholics stand on a cliff. If they go over the edge, they are in trouble. But the overeater's problem is more like being on a slippery hilltop with steep, but not vertical, slopes. Exactly where the danger point starts is hard to figure out. In addition, the further alcoholics get away from the edge of the cliff, the safer they are, but for overeaters it's possible to go too far and end up undereating. Furthermore, an overeater never really knows where the top of the hill is because there is so much confusion about proper nutrition.

❧ The many views of nutrition

The field of nutrition is controversial. While we generally agree that we need certain essential vitamins and minerals, the proper method of eating for compulsive overeaters is open to debate. We are continually bombarded with conflicting information about whether certain foods—ranging from coffee to cholesterol to candy—are appropriate for us.

Everyone seems to have personal views on the issue, and most people feel free to express them loudly. This section presents many of the differing views within the fellowship about what to eat, including my own. I am sure that we will continue to learn more over the coming years, both from the results of scientific research and from our own experience.

Since the only requirement for OA membership is a desire to stop overeating compulsively, the fellowship includes people with every type of food and weight history. There are some who used to weigh five hundred pounds and others who were never obese but who abused food by vomiting or taking laxatives. There are those who grew up fat and those whose eating disorder waited until later in life to strike. There are those, too, who have flip-flopped between anorexia and overeating. OA members also come from many different socioeconomic and religious backgrounds.

The point is that despite our common problem with compulsive overeating, we are individuals with individual needs. No one method of eating could possibly be correct for all of us. Nor is the best method for one person today necessarily the best method for that person a year from now.

Fortunately, OA isn't a diet club and doesn't publish an official OA diet. After all, diets are *temporary* plans for losing weight. And most of us have discovered that we have lost the ability to diet for any length of time. Even when we could stick to a diet until we lost all the weight we wanted to lose, we couldn't keep the weight off. Gloomy statistics confirm that most dieters fail to achieve a lasting weight loss.

❦ Eating sanely

What we need is a sane way of eating—one that doesn't abuse our bodies, one that we can live with for a lifetime. We need to eat just the amount of food our bodies need, no more and no less. In other words, we need to refrain from compulsive overeating. This is called *abstinence.*

You will hear abstinence mentioned continually at OA meetings. After all, abstinence is what we go there for. We have discovered that if we are eating properly, the weight virtually takes care of itself. This doesn't mean that we will never have to think about food. Far from it—we have to pay very careful attention to the physical side of our disease or we will suffer. But we can let go of the obsession with weight and calories that haunted us before OA.

My abstinence is the most important thing to me without exception—because my life is on the line. Some people may claim that their family or that God is more important. All I know is that I am of no use to anyone when I am bingeing my brains out. I also find it very difficult to pray with my mouth full. There is no way that I can be helpful to my family or to humanity if I commit suicide by overeating.

Since abstaining is a life-and-death matter, most of us have quite strong views on what to eat and what not to eat. Controversies over food plans have plagued the fellowship for many years, and the arguments have sometimes grown intense. Those who are so sensitive to a certain food that they can't eat it may resent those who appear to tolerate it. Many in the program are understandably disturbed by the murky definition of abstinence, since what one may call abstinence another may call bingeing.

Some individual beliefs about food have a theological ring to them: this is the only true way of eating and every other way is wrong. Overeaters Anonymous is nonsectarian with respect to food plans. As an organization, we don't pretend to know the appropriate food plan for each of our over 150,000 members, so the final decision about what to eat is left to each person. OA doesn't tell us what church to attend for our spiritual recovery, and it doesn't tell us which food plan is best for our physical recovery. We will have to make our own decisions, but we can learn from the experience of other OA members.

But how does this concept of abstinence translate into the food that I actually eat? How do I know what to eat or how much to eat? There is a large gray area between violent self-destructive eating and perfect nutrition. This makes determining what abstinence is a tricky thing. As one member says, "I don't know what abstinence is, but I know when I've lost it."

This uncertainty can lead to nagging doubts about our food. It's all too easy for our disease to ambush us with thoughts like *I'm not doing it right! Is it really okay for me to eat dairy products even though they are a binge food for other overeaters? Are my vegetable portions too big? Too small? Should I weigh and measure? Should I stop weighing and measuring? Am I getting enough fiber?* There is always something we can beat ourselves up with. An OA friend says choosing what to eat is like taking target practice when you can't see the target: the point isn't how close you get to the bull's-eye, but that you don't shoot yourself with your own gun.

❦ Being honest

The main thing is that you must be honest with yourself about what you are eating, and about whether or not it's working for you. If it's not working, you need the honesty, willingness, and courage to find out what will work and then do it. One fantastic thing about the fellowship is that most members are willing to share their own experience so that other members don't have to repeat their mistakes.

How do OA members abstain from overeating and select a food plan? In the end, each person makes his or her own decision and each person judges his or her own abstinence. Many definitions of abstinence are far too murky for easy implementation. OA sayings such as "abstaining from compulsive overeating," "guilt-free eating," and "sane eating" give little guidance about what to eat and when to eat it. Furthermore, given the ways our addicted brain justifies and rationalizes the most bizarre eating patterns, it helps most of us to adopt working guidelines for our food.

❦ Recognizing the middle ground

Newcomers often confuse abstinence with the "death-camp diet." For so many years, we were either starving or bingeing and recognized no middle ground. Thus, some of us thought that if we weren't bingeing, we had to eat an incredibly small amount of unappetizing food to atone for our past excesses. For example, a newcomer might think that abstinence consists of one hard-boiled egg for breakfast, the sight of a lettuce leaf for lunch, and a whiff of vinegar for dinner. That's not the case! When I sponsor newcomers they are often amazed that I recommend they eat more food than they were planning to eat on their own. Remember that we are trying to develop a way of living and eating that works for the long haul. If we try to restrict our food to ridiculously small portions, we are dooming ourselves to failure.

My working definition of abstinence means that I don't eat between meals and that I don't eat refined sugar. That's my bottom line, and I have been able to stick to it for over a decade. Limiting my eating to three meals a day with no sugar limits the amount of damage I can do in any one day.

Abstinence for others may be more or less restrictive. For example, to a bulimic who has been vomiting five times a day, abstinence may start out as just plain not overeating to the point of wanting to purge. For others, abstinence may mean following their particular food plan to the letter, weighing or measuring everything they eat. Some perfectionists may consider any deviation whatsoever from their food plan a break in their abstinence.

There is a world of difference between eating pounds of junk food and one extra string bean. For some, it's difficult to go from flat-out bingeing to clean abstinence, so it's necessary to proceed gradually on a path away from the old destructive eating patterns. This can best be illustrated by a friend of mine in OA who is a classic sugar-and-starch junkie. Any food that was high in carbohydrates, such as candy or bread, would set up a craving in her for more and lead to overeating. The first thing she did was give up those foods; there was no attempt to limit consumption of any other foods or to stop eating between meals. Gradually, she was able to reduce the quantities of other foods and to limit her eating to regular meals. It took her four years to attain her goal weight, but she has been maintaining a ninety-seven-pound weight loss for over ten years.

OA members eat in a variety of ways. In the end each of us must do what works for us individually. One thing I have noticed, however, is that most successful recovering overeaters have three sets of food disciplines: (1) what to eat, (2) how much to eat, and (3) when to eat. These are decisions we can't avoid making, because we make them, either implicitly or explicitly, every day by the actions we take. Therefore, it's useful to think about these decisions and how we are going to make them.

☀ What to eat

We have known in OA for years that many of us are very sensitive to certain foods. Refined sugar (as well as corn syrup, honey, molasses, fructose, and dextrose) seems to be a major trigger for most overeaters. Many of us also seem to have problems with high-starch foods, such as wheat, rice, and potatoes. Others seem to have problems with oils, butter, and fried foods; still others seem to get turned on by dairy products or salt. We have to be honest with ourselves about what foods (if any) trigger us.

Not only is there the lore that we have built up through our years of experience in OA, but there is now a great deal of scientific evidence that the chemical composition of the foods we eat, particularly the carbohydrate content, affects our moods and thus our behavior. But scientists are still unraveling the details, and we need to make decisions about what we are going to eat today. We can't wait for all the answers, so we must make informed guesses about the proper way of eating based on the experience of other overeaters, on scientific knowledge, on professional guidance, and on common sense.

A good rule of thumb is to avoid any food to which you have a physical sensitivity. Even if you can manage to eat it sometimes without always bingeing, it's good to refrain from it entirely to leave yourself a wide margin of safety. Common sense says that if a particular food does bad things to you, then don't eat it. It's easier to eat none at all than just a little bit, since not taking the first bite prevents a craving for more. If you want to be free from food cravings, don't eat any foods that produce them. Remember, "One bite is too many and a thousand aren't enough."

Only you can decide what your trigger foods are, but it's more than likely that they are your old binge foods. Foods containing refined sugar and alcoholic beverages are problems for most compulsive overeaters. You will have a hard time recovering if you have any trigger foods in your food plan.

Read ingredients labels carefully. Even foods that look healthy or are labeled "natural" or "diet" may contain substances that interfere with your recovery. Natural forms of sugar such as honey, molasses, and brown sugar are still sugar and can be just as harmful as refined sugar. A good rule of thumb is to avoid any food that has sugar in it unless it's fifth or below on the ingredients list. Since food labels rank ingredients by weight, having sugar listed fifth or below means that the quantity is usually small enough to avoid triggering the compulsion. But when in doubt, leave it out.

Use fresh instead of processed food whenever possible. Highly processed food often contains ingredients to which we may be sensitive. For example, some canned fruits are packed in heavy sugar syrups, and most so-called nondairy creamers are loaded with corn syrup solids, which are a problem for many of us. Also, the procedures used to process some foods may lead to a loss in vitamin content.

❦ How much to eat

We all know, even though we hate to admit it, that if we eat too much food we will suffer. Therefore, we need to figure out how much to eat.

For normal people this is no problem. Their bodies correctly monitor their nutritional situation and send them accurate messages about how much to eat. If they eat more than they need, their bodies will automatically compensate. They will naturally desire less food later, or they will burn up the extra energy as heat or activity. They have an "appestat" (like a thermostat) that magically balances their food intake with their energy expenditure, although the exact biological systems involved aren't well understood.

Unfortunately for us, our appestats don't seem to work very well. Why? Who knows. But the question here isn't why, it's what are we going to do about it? A lot depends on how severely your appestat is malfunctioning. If your eating disorder isn't too advanced, you may be able to learn how to trust your appetite about how much to eat. In OA, this is generally called *moderate mealing*—basically you just eat moderate wholesome meals and stop when you've had enough. This doesn't work for everyone in OA. For many of us, we don't really know how much is enough or too much. Eating as much as we want results in disaster. Just using our eyes or stomachs to measure our food can lead to major miscalculations. A food scale, measuring spoons, and a measuring cup are useful devices to ensure that we eat enough without eating too much.

Some people in OA have told me rather forcefully that if I just learned how to love myself, get in touch with my feelings, or trust God, that I would be able to trust my natural God-given appetite to tell me what to eat and what not to eat. But I feel that my appetite is a lot like my 20/800 vision—far from perfect. I can barely see without my glasses, only fuzzy images. If I were to trust my unaided vision when I drove my car, I would quickly get into an accident. My appetite is the same way: I have a very fuzzy sense of enough; it's not precise or accurate. If I were to trust my unaided appetite, I would quickly gain my weight back, because I don't know the meaning of full or the meaning of hungry. I regularly use a scale and a measuring cup to keep from making too many mistakes.

We in OA have debated for a long time about the appropriate method for ensuring that we eat the right amount of food, and we will probably continue to debate it among ourselves for a long time. The bottom line is that you have to do what works for you. If moderate mealing works for you, then do it, but don't expect it to work for everyone. My observation is that moderate mealing works for some of those people who were moderately obese, but not very well for those who were morbidly obese. I tried it and found it a great way to gain weight quickly, so I returned to weighing and measuring most of my food.

I have also found that many in OA don't have any real objections to weighing or measuring food. We just hate to eat less. During our overeating days, many of us were amateur bakers who weighed and measured the ingredients we put into our binge foods all the time. When I was making cookies, I had the most level measuring cups on the planet.

Whether you use a measuring cup or not, there is still the decision of how much to eat. Since individual needs vary, this is where the services of a professional nutritionist or dietitian can come in handy. You can also talk to others in the program. Finding out what works and doesn't work for other overeaters can provide tremendous insight.

Calories count, but we don't count them. You will notice that there is one thing most of us in OA don't do—we don't count calories. In our dieting days, we often kept track of our calories obsessively. We would substitute candy for a meal, thinking it was okay because the number of calories was the same. We would hoard our calorie allotment and blow it on some "treat," or we would start borrowing against future meals until our caloric debt was so high that we junked the diet. Counting calories tends to make us even more obsessed with food.

Instead of counting calories, we plan in advance to eat appropriate amounts of food at reasonable times. If we focus on calories alone, we start to believe that all calories are alike to our bodies. But all calories aren't alike. Remember, we need to eat a balanced diet that gives us the right amount of vitamins, minerals, and amino acids. We need to keep track of more than just calories to make sure we are eating properly. Fifty calories of broccoli and fifty calories of chocolate both have fifty calories, but they have extremely different amounts of the nutrients that our bodies need. Furthermore, they have different effects on our brain chemistry.

❦ *When to eat*

By making a decision not to eat between planned mealtimes, we don't have to spend time asking ourselves, *Should I or shouldn't I?* when food becomes available. Instead, we can tell ourselves, *It's just not feeding time yet! Soon, I'll get my next meal and know that it has just the right amount of food for my well-being.* No one ever died of starvation between lunch and dinner.

Many OA members eat three meals a day, but this is just a suggestion. Some, particularly hypoglycemics, feel that they function better on several small meals a day.

❦ *More suggestions*

In addition to thinking about what to eat, how much to eat, and when to eat, other suggestions about the physical side of our disease are passed on within the fellowship. This section passes on some of this lore to you.

Select a sound food plan and stick to it. Abusing our bodies with excess food, as well as bingeing and then starving, left us in a mental fog about food and our other problems. We have found that stopping the food abuse leads to clearer thinking. A food plan that contains too much or too little food, or one that doesn't give us all the essential vitamins and minerals we need, or one that contains foods that we are sensitive to, will keep us in this fog and make recovery very difficult, if not impossible. Ask other overeaters what food plans worked for them, and don't hesitate to get competent medical advice if you have special needs.

Remember that you have the right to change your food plan whenever you need to, although it's a good idea to discuss it with another OA member first. If you try one food plan, you aren't stuck with it for the rest of eternity. For most of us, our food plans evolve over time as we try different ideas and discover what does and doesn't work for us individually. Few of us eat exactly the same way now as we ate five years ago. As time goes on, conditions change; certain foods go in and out of season or we move to places where different foods are available. Our health may change and require us to eat differently. Most of us make minor modifications in our food plan as we try different things, sticking with what works and getting rid of what doesn't.

Plan your meals in advance. The worst time for us to plan a meal is right at mealtime when we may be fatigued and hungry. At such times, our thinking is often faulty. Planning meals in advance, one day at a time, allows us to make sure that we have the food defrosted (if necessary) and ready to eat when the time comes. Many OA members write down what they plan to eat each day.

One area in which our experience differs from typical diet advice is that we have discovered there is no such thing as "free" food. Even low-calorie foods such as carrots, celery, and popcorn are risky between meals because they keep the hand-to-mouth action going and often lead to a craving for more food. We are seeking a way of life beyond food, and if we continually stuff our faces—even with low-calorie food—sooner or later we will be stuffing our faces with high-calorie junk.

Discuss your food with other people. Many OA members, especially newcomers, discuss what they are eating with other OA people on a regular, often daily, basis. This is especially helpful when planning for tricky situations such as eating at parties or restaurants. Finding out how others abstain from overeating in those situations can help us abstain.

Also, committing what we plan to eat to a sponsor makes it much easier to stick to our plan. But sponsors are good for more than just guidance on food; they can lead us through all areas of the recovery process, right up to the level of their own recovery.

Don't skip meals. How many times have we set ourselves up for a binge by skipping a meal and then "rewarding" ourselves with junk later? When we go too long without food, not only do we get tired and irritable, but our thinking gets cloudy and we are more likely to make poor food choices. We deserve to pamper ourselves by making sure that we get fed regularly.

An old program slogan is HALT: Don't get too Hungry, Angry, Lonely, or Tired. Our thinking gets confused when we feel this way; it's easy for us to make bad decisions about food as well as other things.

Sane, rational eating is what abstinence is all about. Abstinence from compulsive overeating isn't deprivation; rather it frees us from the bondage of our food obsession. The knowledge that we are eating what is right for us removes the mental anguish and leads to guilt-free eating. If we are abstaining from compulsive overeating, we have a right to eat our meals without guilt. Remember, we aren't bad people getting good, but sick people getting better.

❦ *Artificial sweeteners*

Many newcomers wonder about artificial sweeteners. There has been a great debate for years about whether artificial sweeteners such as saccharin or aspartame are safe and whether they are useful for weight reduction. Once again, OA takes a neutral position and leaves decisions about artificial sweeteners up to the individual—as it does all food decisions. Many overeaters with well-established recoveries use them and many don't.

As an old sponsor of mine once told me, "I don't care whether or not the stuff causes cancer in mice or humans. Common sense tells me that any chemical that's so powerful it's 180 times sweeter than sugar can't possibly be totally benign for people like me." You must choose for yourself what chemicals you put into your body. As for myself, I used to drink massive quantities of diet soda. For me, it was like methadone for my sugar addiction. I was still addictively seeking that sweet taste, but it helped me get off the sugar and onto a way of eating that was much better than before. I doubt that I could have given up the artificial sweeteners at the same time I gave up sugar. Eventually, I realized that "sugar in drag" (as some call artificial sweeteners) was leading me away from my recovery and back toward overeating, so I was able to let go of it. I haven't used chemical sweeteners and sugarless gum for over eight years.

❦ *Dietitians and nutritionists*

In OA, we strongly recommend that members get competent professional services when they need it. Once again, we as a group aren't trained as doctors, dietitians, or therapists, and we don't compete with them. But a word of warning is in order if you are looking for nutritional advice. In many states, licensing is loosely regulated. Anyone who wants to call him- or herself a nutritionist can do so without having to take special training or pass certification exams. I have heard stories of some bizarre quacks who set themselves up as self-styled nutritionists.

Whenever you engage the services of a professional, find out where he or she was trained and what makes him or her competent to dispense the advice you are seeking. Also, remember that training in one area doesn't make one an expert in another. For example, a doctor may be a very good heart surgeon but may have had little training in nutrition or eating disorders. Some professionals, although technically competent, don't seem to comprehend eating disorders and have trouble understanding our needs.

When considering the services of a professional nutritionist, talk to some of the clients. For example, find out whether all clients get the same diagnosis. Some nutritionists have a reputation for declaring that all their patients have the same problem—such as hypoglycemia, yeast infection, candida, or certain allergies—and need the same food plan. Make sure that the person you hire will treat you as an individual.

Also, be aware that new information about diet and nutrition is being discovered every day, and that the recommendations from authorities in the field change accordingly. Here is an example: For a long time the accepted word was that fat is bad and can lead to heart disease. Then came evidence that Native Alaskans, who traditionally live on a high-fat diet, suffer from low rates of heart disease. The explanation seems to be that the *type* of fat is extremely important, not just the amount. In order to figure out what is best for you, temper the recommendations you receive with common sense and your personal experience.

Don't be surprised if your nutritionist tells you things you already know. Most of us have read plenty of books on dieting and nutrition. We know that to lose weight we need to take in fewer calories than we burn up (which usually means eat less and exercise more), eat a limited amount of fat, and generally avoid empty calories. Still, a nutritionist can help us analyze our food plan and spot potential trouble areas.

And don't be surprised if your nutritionist can't seem to comprehend the addictive nature of certain foods. Some nutritionists do and some don't. It's difficult for someone who doesn't have an eating disorder to comprehend what it's like. A nutritionist may say that a candy bar now and then won't do much harm (which is indeed true for normal people), but for an addict like me, one candy bar usually leads to a second and a third and so forth. I am much better off not taking that first bite.

❦ Exercise

Exercise is a frequent topic in many books and discussions of weight reduction. All of our lives, people (who, usually, have never been fat) have been telling us that we should eat less and exercise more. We have attempted and abandoned countless exercise programs. Our basements are resting places for a variety of unused exercise equipment. Many of us have been tortured in physical education classes led by sadistic, would-be drill instructors who delighted in humiliating us. And then there was the humiliation that our classmates inflicted on us in the locker room.

Moderate exercise is an essential part of recovering from an eating disorder. My observation is that everyone I know with a good recovery gets plenty of physical activity, whether they are willing to call it exercise or not.

You won't hear a lot about exercise at OA meetings. As one OA member put it, "The best exercise I can do today is to run up and down the Twelve Steps." We put the focus on restructuring our life so that we don't overeat. And we find that the desire to exercise is a natural by-product of our recovery. Most recovering overeaters find a way to include reasonable physical activity in their lives. For most of us, however, losing the weight *allowed* us to exercise, rather than the other way around. When I was a hundred pounds heavier, climbing a flight of steps was a major endeavor. Attempts at more severe exertion, such as running, could have caused major injury to my ankles, knees, and back.

Many of us have also used exercise as another whip with which to beat ourselves. It was just like the crazy diets and fasts—a way to punish ourselves for overeating. We don't have to calculate how many miles we have to run to burn off food if we don't eat it to begin with. As one OA member put it, "Thank God I don't have to jog anymore."

Many of us treated exercise the way we treated the fad diets we used to try. We would avoid it like the plague, and then we would overdo it. Eventually, the novelty wore off and we would stop. In OA, we are trying to develop a sustainable way of life, not a temporary spurt of activity that we can't keep up.

Here are a few hints: (1) Start easy. Devoting just a few minutes a day to physical activity is a good way to start. If you overdo it at first, you won't be able to sustain it. (2) Get some professional advice from a doctor before you take up anything strenuous. (3) Take it one day at a time. Soon you will find out for yourself what everyone else has been saying—that exercise makes you feel better.

❦ The scale

The traditional OA suggestion is to weigh yourself once a month when losing weight and once a week while maintaining it. Weighing yourself too frequently doesn't tell you anything that you don't already know; you know what you have been eating and how well your clothes fit. Weighing every day won't make the weight come off any faster, but it does make it easy to play mind games with yourself: If the numbers are low, celebrate by eating. If the numbers are high, console yourself by eating. And so forth and so on. The mental anguish caused by weighing yourself too frequently doesn't help. Your self-worth doesn't need to depend on the scale.

Weighing yourself too infrequently isn't good either. It's very easy to gradually develop sloppy eating practices within abstinence that will lead to an undesired weight gain. Stepping on the scale regularly is one way to minimize denial and identify sloppy practices before they become serious.

Weighing yourself at least once a month but not more than once a week seems to be a good compromise between over- and underweighing. Many women, to account for cyclical fluctuations, prefer to weigh themselves at the same time in their menstrual cycle.

❧ *How to figure out your goal weight*

Since I had never weighed my goal weight before, I didn't know what it should be. A quick look at those infamous life insurance charts reveals a large range of acceptable weights for several different frame sizes. *Gee, do I really have a large frame? Or is that my denial talking?* Figuring out where to put yourself on those charts can be a tricky exercise.

A common trap is to set an unrealistically low goal weight. Remember, any weight loss that gets you out of a health risk is fine. Any weight loss beyond that is just cosmetic. Many people think that they should weigh what their skinniest friend weighed in high school. Wrong. Scientists now think that the range of desirable body weights increases as you get older.[*] Some OA members set a low goal because they want to have a few extra pounds "in the bank" just in case they relapse, but that can lead to several serious health risks.

If you become underweight, your body may respond by turning up your appetite and making it even harder for you to eat sanely. Your body may also become more efficient at holding on to calories and thus slow down your metabolism even further. Or it may try to shut down by becoming cold and lethargic. Women who lose too much weight may have menstrual difficulties and risk their ability to have children.

So how do you figure out how much you should weigh? Next time you visit your doctor, ask for advice, but don't be surprised if you get a vague answer. We may wish to hear a precise number—for example, 131.4159 pounds—but your doctor may say that anything between 125 and 145 is healthy for your age and frame.

Another thing to look at is your body's fat content, which is a more accurate measure of obesity than just weight. Your doctor can do this measurement or can refer you to someone who can. But even this test won't tell you exactly what you should weigh.

Therefore, I recommend choosing several goals. First of all, figure out what the healthy weight range is for you. Aim for the weight that no longer presents a threat to your health from heart disease, diabetes, and so forth. Once there, feel free to experiment with several different weights within that range until you find a safe, comfortable weight where you like your appearance. If your friends start looking concerned and asking if you have been ill, you may have gone too far.

---

[*]National Research Council, *Diet and Health* (Washington D.C., 1989), 564.

☙ OA food plans and the infamous gray sheet

OA used to publish food plans. Since you will undoubtedly hear about them at meetings, a little bit of historical background will help you understand what people are talking about.

In the early days, OA was much more like a diet club and distributed diets, or food plans, to its members. Food plans were often referred to by the color of the paper they were printed on. One very famous food plan is known as the "Gray Sheet," sometimes also known as "Plan A" or "Plan 3." Others were the "Orange Sheet" and the "Blue Sheet." As one old-timer put it, "I've done every food plan from the Gray Sheet to the Bull Sheet."

After many years of heated controversy, OA decided to stop publishing food plans in 1986. This decision didn't mean that it was inherently bad to follow a food plan, just that it was not appropriate for OA to be prescribing one. Given the changing state of current nutritional wisdom and the conflicting advice given by different experts in the field, trying to devise food plans that fit the diverse needs of over 150,000 compulsive overeaters became an impossible task. The collective group conscience decided that offering specific nutritional advice conflicted with Tradition Eight, since nutritional advice is the realm of professionals, and also with Tradition Ten, since dispensing specific nutritional advice could involve us in public controversy.

The decision to abandon food plans was not unanimous, and there was much grumbling about how the decision was made. Many groups, particularly some H.O.W.* groups, continued to hand out food plans for many years. These underground food plans tend to be variants of the old Gray Sheet.

The Gray Sheet was one of the most popular of the old food plans, and it has been a source of continuing controversy long since OA stopped publishing it. The small portions ensured a quick weight loss, and the list of allowable foods omitted most problem foods, making it easier for many OA members to stick with it. Some people damn it as being nutritionally unbalanced; others claim that it was the first way of eating that led to physical relief from the craving to overeat.

The Gray Sheet was a typical high-protein, low-carbohydrate food plan. OA didn't invent it; it followed the traditions of other such diets that were popular in the late 1960s. It's similar to many weight-loss diets in that the large quantity of vegetables on it seem designed to give maximum vol-

---

*H.O.W. (which stands for Honesty, Open-mindedness, and Willingness) groups are OA meetings that have a lot more structure to them than regular OA meetings. Some H.O.W. meetings distribute food plans, which are usually modified versions of the Gray Sheet. Needless to say, these differences have made H.O.W. meetings rather controversial meetings within OA.

ume with minimum calories. It was not necessarily meant for lifelong eating. When a member hit goal weight, the thing to do was to slowly add food until the weight stabilized.

The Gray Sheet has appeared in many forms. After OA stopped publishing it, underground versions began to appear, many with various additions to suit whoever published it. Some of the underground versions are very different from the original.

This section describes what was on most versions of the Gray Sheet. The purpose is not to advocate it, but to let you know what other people are talking about. It's a description, not a prescription. The basic structure of the Gray Sheet was three meals a day with nothing in between, not even the "free foods" from our dieting days, except for black coffee, tea, or diet soda. There was a long list of foods to be avoided, including all the usual binge foods, such as candy, cake, and alcohol, but also bread and bread products. Vitamin supplements were recommended, as were regular medical checkups.

For each of the three meals of the day, the Gray Sheet allowed one protein serving. A protein serving meant four ounces of beef, chicken, or fish after cooking; or two eggs, two ounces of cheese, one cup of plain yogurt, or eight ounces of milk. Breakfast consisted of one protein serving and one fruit serving.

The original Gray Sheet listed allowable fruits and the appropriate serving sizes, such as one medium apple or one cup of strawberries. Fruits high in starch or sugar, such as pears and bananas, were not allowed.

One cup of most cooked vegetables was allowed, and a small amount of butter was allowed in cooking the vegetables. Some vegetables, such as carrots and winter squash, were only allowed in half-cup portions. Very starchy vegetables, such as peas and corn, were not allowed. For lunch, another protein serving was allowed, as well as a vegetable and a "finger salad."

A "finger salad" meant three small raw vegetables, or a salad without dressing. I know some people who interpreted this as meaning three incredibly large carrots. They would eat so many carrots that their skin took on an orange tint. Sometimes you could spot the Gray Sheeters at a meeting by checking for orange hands. Dinner consisted of another protein serving, a vegetable, and a salad.

A salad consisted of two cups of salad-type vegetables such as lettuce and mushrooms, with two tablespoons of dressing. Stories abound in OA about people going to great lengths to cram as much into the measuring cup as possible.

Compared with some diets of its era, there was quite a bit of flexibility in terms of the specific fruits, vegetables, and proteins allowed on the plan.

In general, it tended to come in at around 1200 calories per day, which is reasonable for a weight-loss diet. Problem areas involved calcium intake, which was inadequate if dairy products weren't used as part of the protein servings. Also, daily intake of the Vitamins B and E was marginal, which led to the recommendation for vitamin supplements.

How not to eat:
Handling tricky situations

In OA, we try to develop a new lifestyle that will not only arrest our compulsive overeating, but will also improve our emotional and spiritual lives. We need a lifestyle that's good enough for the long haul and robust enough to withstand anything life can throw at us. But we need to deal with food every day, and OA has developed a lot of nuts-and-bolts practices for getting through these situations.

One thing we stress is the philosophy of one day at a time. We don't have to figure out today what we are going to eat every day for the rest of our lives. We don't have to figure out today how to solve all our problems. All we have to do is concentrate on doing what is in front of us and worry about the future when it arrives. Taking it one day at a time doesn't mean that we become flaky people who never plan. It means that we skip the obsessive worrying about possible future events. For example, we don't need to worry about how to abstain on Thanksgiving until it's time to defrost the turkey.

Sometimes we have to take it one minute or one second at a time; we can survive for a few minutes or hours without our favorite binge foods. The world won't stop if we don't eat *now*. We can concentrate on not overeating now and worry about later *later*. Tolerating a little discomfort for a short time is easier than the thought of a lifetime of discomfort. Cheer up. It does get better. This section offers some techniques for surviving one day at a time in tricky situations.

❦ How to refuse food gracefully
People are always trying to feed us. It's a common social custom to share food with guests, co-workers, friends, and family. Unfortunately, we are often offered too much food or the wrong food at the wrong time. Many of us are afraid of offending our hosts by not eating what they offer. Sometimes we fear they will interpret our saying no as a personal rejection. We need to learn to turn down such offers tactfully. Just remember that no one who truly cares for you wants you to eat in a manner that's harmful to you.

The easiest thing to do is just to say, "No thanks. Not right now." This works 90 percent of the time. I don't go into any long-winded explanations about eating healthy or being on a diet or having an allergy to junk food. I have found that most people are just trying to be polite when they offer food and aren't interested in long explanations of why you don't want it. Furthermore, trying to explain an eating disorder to a person who doesn't have one is like trying to explain color to a blind person.

People turn down food all the time. Why? Because they aren't hungry. And when they aren't hungry, the thought of stuffing food down their throats makes them ill, so they say no. And they don't make a big deal of it. So when people offer me food at inappropriate times, I just say no. If I don't make a big deal of it, no one else will.

I almost never say, "I am on a special diet." That requires a long explanation. Besides, our friends have seen us pretending to be on diets before when we wanted excuses to break them. Often, they will think that we are looking for excuses to eat, so they will provide one: "Oh come on, it's only one!" Or, "This is low-calorie fudge! It's only four calories per gram!" So many times we have said, "Oh, I really shouldn't," when the message we were really sending was, "I really want to but I want you to give me a good excuse so I don't lose face and can blame you if I don't stick to my diet." A polite but firm "No thanks" doesn't send this kind of mixed message.

Also, mentioning that you are on a diet may make dieting the topic of conversation, which can sometimes be most unpleasant. After having my body size be a public issue all of my life, I am tired of talking about dieting with people who don't seem to understand.

Occasionally, you will encounter someone who is a bit more persistent. My next line of defense is a white lie such as "I'm not hungry yet" or "I just had lunch." That usually does the trick. After all, food really doesn't do much good for a person who isn't hungry. "Maybe later" is another good line that usually defuses the situation. By putting it off, there is a good chance that the food will run out or the host will forget about it. Just remember that if you don't make a big deal of it, most of the time no one else will either.

Getting an invitation to dinner at someone's home is a bit trickier, since you are expected to eat what is served. Then, I make a discreet inquiry as to what will be served: "I would love to have dinner at your place. Do you have any idea what you will be serving?" If it sounds like I can get my usual food from the planned menu, I say nothing further. On the other hand, if the planned menu is something like deep-fried ice cream with chocolate sauce, I say, "Hmmm." That usually prompts the host to ask if I have any special preferences or dietary requirements, and I respond with a quick description of the way I eat. Since most hosts will bend over backward to please their guests, this usually presents no problem. If there are still problems, however, here are several alternatives: (1) you can offer to bring your own food to spare your host the bother of preparing special food for you; (2) you can turn the invitation around and invite them to your place for dinner so you will have control over the menu; or (3) you can meet in a restaurant where you will be able to order what you want.

❦ Restaurants

Restaurants provided many of us with a handy excuse to overeat, either because they were associated with special occasions or because the fact that someone else prepared the food somehow took the responsibility for our eating away from us. Many of us did some of our worst eating in restaurants, and we may now feel threatened in an environment where food is so plentiful. Sometimes I get the feeling that restaurants are conspiring to either fatten me up, starve me, poison me, or bankrupt me.

Relax. The key to successful abstaining in restaurants is to remember that our bodies don't care where the food comes from. There is no reason to deviate from sane and rational eating because we are away from our own kitchens. Just because the food is in front of us doesn't mean we have to eat it.

Abstaining in restaurants starts with selecting the right restaurant. Although you can abstain anywhere, it will be easier if you go to a restaurant that has a wide selection of good food. Some restaurants appear never to have heard of green vegetables and fresh fruit. Don't go to them. Use common sense when you order. The Sweet and Sour Fried Starch with Chocolate Sauce is going to be loaded with sugar, starch, grease, and salt, and is certainly not what sane eating is about. If you have any questions about how your food is prepared, most restaurants will be happy to tell you. Don't be afraid to ask for food that's prepared the way you need it—without sugar or other ingredients to which you might be sensitive.

I usually give restaurants the benefit of the doubt when it comes to what they put in their food. But if there is something in the food that sets off a craving for more, I will know it. It may be painful to get through the rest of the day without overeating, but I have the tools of the program to help me through. Whenever I am taught such a painful lesson, I don't go back to that restaurant again or don't order that dish again. My serenity is too important to spend my time fighting food cravings.

Controlling portions can be a problem in restaurants. It's unlikely that you will eat the same quantities in a restaurant as you would at home, so it can be tempting to order and eat more than you need. I have found that most restaurant portions for salads and vegetables are much too small for my liking, but their protein portions are larger than I usually eat. The bottom line is that you must be honest with yourself about what you are eating. If you eat too much, you will suffer! If portion control in restaurants is a problem for you, take your scale and measuring cup with you or eat at home.

Salad bars and buffets provide another temptation for overeaters. On the one hand, they are often the only source of wholesome food in places like fast-food restaurants, but having the opportunity to serve ourselves as much as we want can be a real temptation. What I usually do is decide that one full plate (unless the plate is very small) is a meal, and I don't go back for seconds. A lot of the foods at buffets and salad bars are loaded with sugar, such as the Jell-O and other desserts. When at a salad bar or buffet, eat the same types of foods that you would at home, and eat no more than you would at home.

The management wants you to be happy, have a good time, and come back. Your server is usually willing to get you what you want because you will then leave a good tip. But you must tell those who serve you what you want or they will guess. And they usually guess wrong. Be polite but assertive, and you will get the abstinent food you need.

❦ *Parties*

Parties can be especially threatening to overeaters, since there is food all around and it seems like everyone is eating it and having a good time. There is no reason for us to avoid parties or any other social occasion, if, as it says in the Big Book, *"we have a legitimate reason for being there."** We don't have to be hermits to recover from overeating. We don't have to shy away from our friends just because there might be food. Indeed, the purpose of our program is to allow us to live life as fully as possible; enjoying social events without self-destructing by overeating is part of recovery.

I have noticed that when other people put things in their mouths, I want to put things in my mouth. So I make sure I have at least a glass of water to drink from.

If the food starts calling to you at the party, remember that you have a whole kit of tools to call upon. You can excuse yourself and make a phone call, or go to the bathroom and pray. Excess food won't do you any good. It won't put dollars in your bank account, it won't get you the mate you always wanted, and it won't make feelings of shyness go away. Remember that you aren't obligated to stay for the entire party. Parties are for having a good time; they aren't meant to be endurance contests. It's okay to arrive late and leave early.

Be careful when you get home from the party. Many of us were quite skilled at appearing to diet in front of others and then bingeing secretly by ourselves. These "old tapes" may start playing when we get home. Our insane thinking may tell us to "reward" ourselves with food because we didn't abuse food at the party.

---

*Alcoholics Anonymous, 101.

❧ Potlucks

Potlucks can be harder than normal parties. One is normally expected to bring food to share with others, which can seem very threatening to someone for whom a structured food plan is working well.

One thing I do for potlucks is to make sure I bring enough food for me to have a complete meal in case I choose not to eat anything the others have brought. Potlucks are notorious for poor coordination: I once went to a potluck where at least half of the people brought dessert. Thus, I plan for not finding anything I can eat. If there is wholesome food there, then I am pleasantly surprised and usually substitute it for the food I brought.

❧ Holidays

Holidays are a challenge on several levels: parties and ritual feasts may tempt us to break our abstinence, family gatherings may bring up unresolved family problems, and holiday traveling makes following our food plan more difficult. Keep in mind that our disease never takes a holiday; it's always looking for an excuse to reactivate itself. Once we start overeating, we never know how long it may take to stop.

I have heard many people say that a one-day binge triggered a relapse that lasted for months or years. You will be much happier after the holidays if you stay abstinent during them. It's a great relief for me to approach each January without remorse over my holiday eating and without the dreaded first-Monday-in-January diet hanging over my head.

Your first abstinent holidays may seem rough, but you can enjoy them for what they celebrate rather than see them as an excuse to overeat. If you are invited to a holiday feast, remember that no one is going to tie you up and force food down your throat. Talk to other OA members about how they abstained in similar situations. Remember that those who truly love you will support you in your recovery from your eating disorder.

In many areas, there are special OA holiday meetings. Take advantage of them. If there aren't any in your area, make sure you get to a regular OA meeting to talk with others about your plans for surviving the holidays.

One more word of advice: skip holiday baking. Some newcomers to OA have the mistaken idea that baking traditional holiday junk food for their families is a way of showing love for them. Feeding your loved ones empty calories and training them in bad nutritional habits isn't showing love, it is abusive. I have seen overeaters who tried to eat vicariously through their families, and almost inevitably they got back into overeating themselves. We aren't doing ourselves or our families any good by wallowing in the food in the kitchen. Even if we don't eat the food we bake, being exposed to its sight and smell for several hours or days drains our serenity. If your family wants junk food, let them get their own. They know where to get it.

❦ Halloween

Halloween is a slippery day for a lot of us. When I was a kid, it was my favorite day of the year. I could get tons and tons of junk food just by asking. It was so great that I kept trick-or-treating until I was twenty years old.

Trick or treat puts us into a tricky situation. Every Halloween an army of kids knock on our door and expect us to give them something. What do we do? Do we give them food of dubious nutritional value and train them in bad nutritional habits? Some of us have grave misgivings about feeding kids substances that we consider unhealthy. On the other hand, we don't want to be grinches who deny the children the fun that they deserve. Who are we to impose our food plan on others?

Some people only give out wholesome food on Halloween. Unfortunately, most wholesome foods, such as apples and oranges, are unwrapped and thus vulnerable to tampering. With all the stories about poisoned Halloween treats, no sane parent would allow a child to accept unpackaged food from a stranger. Why give something that will be thrown out?

One solution is to give money instead of junk food. Kids love it! They already get enough junk food on Halloween, so another candy bar means little to them. Handing out a quarter puts a bigger smile on a kid's face than a candy bar. They can use the money to buy exactly what they want. Money is never the wrong flavor; it doesn't cause tooth decay and doesn't go stale.

Even more important, you won't have to worry about the temptation of having junk food around the house. How many times have we stocked up on Halloween treats only to eat them all before Halloween? And how many times did we, either consciously or unconsciously, buy too much junk so that we could have lots of leftovers? Leftovers will certainly not be a problem if we give out money!

❦ Thanksgiving

The biggest ritual feast of all is Thanksgiving. For us, Turkey Day is Amateur Day because it's the one day of the year when the rest of the population tries to eat the way we ate year-round. The difference is that other people stop overeating the next day. We couldn't.

I remember many Thanksgivings when I stuffed my face along with the rest of my family. But soon after the meal, when they would be occupied with other things, I would want more food and would find myself in the kitchen picking at the carcass of the turkey. My mother was amazed at how quickly I would come begging for the next meal.

Remember that we are people who have lost control of our overeating. If we could have stopped overeating whenever we wanted to, we would never have reached the low points that we did. We don't have the option of having a quick binge and getting back on track again. Many times we thought we would make an exception for "just this one special occasion," only to discover that suddenly every day became another special occasion that demanded we stuff our bodies with unneeded food.

❦ Christmas and other winter days

The best present you can give yourself for Christmas (or any other day, for that matter) is to take care of your body. Pamper yourself by making sure you get just the right amount of nutritious food for optimal health—not too much and not too little. The dark gloomy days of winter are depressing enough. They will be even more depressing if you get back into the food.

The winter holidays are hard not only because of family events and traveling, but also because of the winter darkness. I believe that humans have been conditioned to react to our natural environment. When it gets dark at night, our bodies sense that the day is over and that it's time to sleep. When the sun comes up, our bodies sense that it's time to wake up. Many of us intuitively judge the passage of time by the sun. When it goes down in the evening our bodies say, "Time to knock off work and get some dinner." But in the fall the sun sets earlier and earlier, and by the start of winter it seems as if it has disappeared entirely. Thus, our bodies may start telling us to have dinner hours before we had planned, making it easy to confuse these body signals with a legitimate need for food. I believe this is one of the reasons why so many of us did our worst bingeing in the late afternoons and early evenings.

So what can you do about it? Just knowing that the craving is brought on by the season makes it easier to deal with. You know that it will pass, and you can use all the other tools of the program to help get through until dinnertime. Instead of reaching for a snack, you can reach for the phone and talk to another overeater who may be going through the same thing. Perhaps there is an OA meeting that you can attend at that yucky time of the day when the craving is at its worst.

❦ Business meals

Some overeaters fear that if they refuse food in a business environment it will harm their careers. Nothing could be further from the truth. The sad fact of life today is that fat people are perceived as weak. Now that I have lost the weight and hear what normal people say behind fat people's backs, I am convinced that the discrimination against fat people in business is far worse than I had ever dreamed!

Indeed, eating properly indicates that you are in control. It means that you care enough about yourself and the image you present to make sure that you get the proper food you need. Demonstrating control over your food conveys a sense of discipline and power that's a tremendous asset in the business world.

I joined OA and lost the weight while working for a major West Coast energy company. Since then, I have worked for several consulting firms. I have traveled around the world on business, and I have entertained clients on expense accounts while abstaining. My latest employers were unaware of my eating disorder. I didn't say anything about my weight history or the way I ate (thank God for anonymity); I just kept on abstaining in my normal way. Eventually, my co-workers noticed that I ate sanely and rationally and that I always declined offers for junk food. I became known as the "man with the iron will." Little did they know! I always chuckled when they said that because I knew that my will had totally failed, and that I still needed five OA meetings a week to keep me sane.

In a business setting, I usually don't volunteer any information about my style of eating unless I think I can do some good by telling someone about OA. I just order an abstinent meal from the menu. If asked about my food, I just say in a matter-of-fact way that I am careful about what I eat—and leave it at that.

When the gang goes out drinking in bars, I join them and guzzle a lot of mineral water. They are amazed that I can have a good time, still drive home, and not be ill the next day. This does wonders for one's reputation for responsibility.

❦ Travel

Travel can also be threatening. At home, we know where the OA meetings are, whom we can call, and where to get the wholesome food we need. All this changes when we travel. For many of us, vacations meant that it was okay for us to eat anything we wanted to. We remembered places not because of what we did or saw, but because of what we ate. Our eating disorder goes with us wherever we go. The nature of our compulsion is such that if we overeat, we never know how long it will take us to regain our abstinence, if ever. Therefore, it's of utmost importance that we take whatever steps necessary to make sure that we don't return to the living hell of compulsive overeating. It's possible to abstain quite easily when traveling. The key is to remember that if you fail to plan, you plan to fail.

Working a program when you are traveling requires that you plan to continue to work the tools and Steps of the program while you are on the road. Just remember that the basic principle of OA is that we help ourselves when we try to help other overeaters, so it's important to maintain contact with other OA members while traveling.

I have traveled over a hundred thousand miles through at least half of the fifty states and over a dozen countries while abstaining. Here are some of the techniques that I have found helpful.

Meetings, literature, tapes, postcards. If you know ahead of time where you are going, find out where the OA meetings are at your destination. Write or call the World Service Office for this information. For $10, they will send you a copy of the International Meeting Directory, which lists every OA meeting in the world, complete with the telephone numbers of people to contact.

If you don't have enough lead time to find out where the meetings are in advance, look up OA in the phone book when you get to your destination. If you can't find OA, try AA to see if they know where any OA meetings are held.

Getting to OA meetings away from home is a vital way to stay sane through all the hassles of traveling. Just remember to call the contact numbers provided by the World Service Office before you try to locate a meeting. This will ensure that you get up-to-date directions on how to get to the meeting and avoid disappointment if the meeting has been moved or canceled.

Don't forget the other OA tools while you are on the road. Pack some of the literature. It will really help you maintain your sanity when your flight has been delayed and you have nothing to do for eight hours in a strange airport. Long-distance phone calls cost money, but they are usually cheaper than food. Postcards to your OA friends back home help both you and them.

Eating on the road. Your food supply can become uncertain on the road. But with a little planning, you can usually get what you need. Most towns have grocery stores and restaurants; just make sure to leave enough time in your schedule to find them. Grocery store and restaurant hours vary considerably from city to city, but if worst comes to worst, you can usually find something edible at a convenience store.

It's often helpful to carry backup food when traveling in case it's inconvenient or impossible to get to a store or restaurant. I usually carry food like a can of tuna fish (don't forget a can opener). Fruits and vegetables will keep for a few days without refrigeration. If you are driving, take an ice chest along. Most hotels and motels will refrigerate your food (such as the morning yogurt) if you ask them. It often helps if you put the food in a paper bag with your name on it. Be pleasant but assertive when you ask. Remember that these establishments want to be helpful so you will come back. If the clerk at the front desk doesn't know how to fulfill your request, try the bar, coffee shop, or room service associated with the hotel.

Airlines. Airline travel represents several challenges that can be overcome with a little advance planning. For example, you may find yourself at thirty thousand feet at mealtime with no food in sight. Or you may not have time to get a proper meal at the airport restaurant during your stopover between flights. Packing a meal in advance is one way to guarantee that the food you need will be available when you need it.

Be prepared for the fact that some flight attendants will walk down the aisle and throw snacks at you without even asking you if you want any. Just say "No thanks" and hand (or throw, if need be) the snacks back to them. Don't tempt fate by holding on to the snacks as potential "presents" for others.

The air in an airliner is very dry and it's easy to get dehydrated. Since people like us often confuse thirst with hunger, remember to drink plenty of liquids. Plain water is almost always available. When drinks are served, I ask for an entire can of mineral water or club soda so that I don't have to keep asking for refills.

Most airlines will go out of their way to get you the food you need as long as you give them twenty-four hours' advance notice. They usually offer a variety of special meals, including kosher, vegetarian, low-calorie, and more. I have found their diabetic meals are usually the closest to my preferred way of eating.

Don't forget, however, that surprises are to be expected when you travel, especially on an airplane. Plan for each contingency. Sooner or later (usually sooner), the airline will goof up and not provide your special meal. Or your flight will be delayed for five hours and the dinner that you were expecting at 7:00 P.M. won't be served till after midnight. Just remember that you won't starve to death if your meal is delayed a few hours, and that attacking the candy machines at the airport won't do you any good. Being prepared with a backup meal has come in handy for me.

Foreign travel. Foreign travel involves special complications. OA meetings tend to be fewer and farther between in foreign lands. Nevertheless, getting to one can be a real lifesaver. One of my former sponsors was bingeing his way across Europe when he wound up in Paris. It was there that he got abstinent and started a one-hundred-pound weight loss that he has maintained for several years.

Language barriers complicate things in foreign countries. Many times I have played "menu roulette" and wound up with something different from what I was expecting. Here you have to use common sense and good judgment. You know what wholesome food looks like and you know what junk food looks like. When in doubt, leave it out.

Getting your familiar foods may be difficult or impossible in certain countries. Local customs, as well as legal barriers and tariffs, may make some items hard to find or prohibitively expensive. Nevertheless, there is usually a supply of adequate food. Most cities have grocery stores and food stands, and even if you don't know how to speak the language, you still know what wholesome food looks like. Buy a phrase book and dictionary so that you can decipher ingredient lists and find out if the food has been sweetened with *sucre* or *Zucker*. Labeling laws differ from country to country, however, so labels may not always reveal the exact contents of food.

If you are hooked on diet foods, be aware that they may not be readily available abroad, so you may wish to pack enough to last the entire trip. Also, the laws on artificial sweeteners are different abroad—some countries allow artificial sweeteners that are currently illegal in the United States. Some foreign "diet" foods, such as soft drinks, may contain mixtures of sugar and artificial sweeteners, and thus aren't always low in calories.

The small amount of advance planning and additional effort needed to work your program in foreign countries is worth it. By abstaining while traveling, you will have a much better time than if you return to overeating. You won't have to deal with the guilt or the painful experience of growing out of your clothes on the road, and you won't have to struggle to get abstinent again. By attending OA meetings in distant lands, you will meet people that you otherwise wouldn't have met. It will enrich your life; I speak from experience. It's possible to go to Switzerland without eating chocolate, to Germany without drinking beer, and to France without drinking wine—and still have a good time. I know, because I have done it.

❦ Visiting home

Going back home to visit parents can be stressful. Many of us did our worst eating at home, and our parents often know exactly how to push our buttons. After living independently for years, it's difficult if we are treated like children again. We may come from a less than ideal family where alcoholism, overeating, and other addictions are rampant. Some in our families may still be practicing their addictions and may try to drag us down with them.

Don't forget that those who truly care about you will support you in your recovery from your eating disorder. But they may have seen you do so many crazy things over the years that they may think OA is just another one of your phases.

We have sent our family so many mixed messages that they may not know what we really want. There were times I yelled at my mother when she fed me too much junk food, but soon after I would ask her to bake me a batch of fudge.

Working your program at your parents' home is the same as working it elsewhere: Don't overeat. Go to meetings. Work the Steps. Getting away to a meeting can be a good way to cool off when things get touchy. It's also a good way to replenish that reservoir of serenity for those thoughtless questions that relatives sometimes ask, such as "Why aren't you married yet?"

Some of us played the martyr role in our family: *Be nice to poor me because I am on a diet.* We may have expected everyone to stand up and applaud when we stopped killing ourselves with food. We don't have to do that anymore. We no longer need to expect special treatment; we just need to take care of ourselves.

❦ *Reentry syndrome*

After traveling, or after any other stressful experience, watch out for what I call the *reentry syndrome.* I have watched a number of people abstain through extended travels and then start overeating on the way home from the airport. The excitement of our travels sometimes makes us forget about our eating disorder. It's easy while on the road to drift away from our support network and meetings. We may get deluded into thinking that we don't need to go to as many meetings or make as many phone calls as we used to. Amnesia sets in, and we may forget that we need to work with other overeaters in order to survive. But the disease is patient, and when our day-to-day reality returns, the food starts screaming at us.

The best way to deal with reentry syndrome is through prevention. Being aware that it can be a problem helps us avoid it. Attending OA meetings on the road, if possible, keeps us mindful of our recovery and prevents amnesia. Staying in touch with our sponsor and other OA friends, through postcards and phone calls, also helps. If we haven't been able to get to meetings on the road, we need to get to them as soon as we can when we return.

❦ *Physical pain*

All of us suffer from physical pain at one time or another. When in pain, we tend to get in bad moods and we become irritable. But abusing ourselves with too much food is a poor analgesic. Extra food won't make the pain go away. It won't make us heal any faster.

As I write this paragraph, I am suffering from severe back pain. Every now and then my lower back goes into a spasm for a couple of days. Fortunately, these occurrences are a lot less frequent since I lost the weight. Nevertheless, the food isn't calling to me at the moment. Why? I don't know, but I suspect it's because OA works. Through the years I have observed many overeaters endure extreme pain, including years of chronic pain, without overeating. They have proved to me that I am better off if I don't take that first bite, and that I can stay abstinent and happy no matter what life throws at me.

In dealing with pain, we use the same tools of the program that we use to deal with other difficult problems. We pray for guidance. We talk with others to find out how they handled similar situations without overeating. We don't hesitate to seek professional help.

Many professionals are well trained to help with the problem of physical pain. We don't have to practice our old character defect of denial and pretend that our problems will go away if we ignore them. And although some of us are justifiably leery about powerful painkillers that may numb our judgment, we don't have to put on a macho act and neglect medication that could help us heal.

❦ Emotional pain and painful memories

After you put down the food, a lot of painful memories may surface. You may feel guilt for the things you have done and rage for the things that were done to you. Overeating won't change the past. Overeating will only slow down your recovery.

The clarity of mind that comes from abstinence makes it possible to cope with these issues on a new and deeper level. OA provides a variety of tools for dealing with emotional pain and painful memories. Many painful memories are stirred up by the thorough self-examination of the Fourth Step. Using the tool of writing about the feelings that come up is a powerful way to handle them. Talking about the pain with your sponsor or another OA member is a tremendous benefit. Prayer is also good for dealing with lingering resentments.

Some of us have memories of extremely painful events that we aren't sure really happened. What matters now isn't whether they happened, but the pain we feel. A therapist trained in this area can help us resolve the pain. We need to be gentle with ourselves and continue our abstinence.

Some of us are survivors of childhood incest, rape, or other traumatic sexual abuse. Once again, professional therapy is helpful in dealing with the aftereffects of sexual abuse.

Most OA members are sympathetic but inexperienced in handling these issues. One thing we do know is that returning to overeating won't change the past.

❦ Pregnancy and childbirth

As a male, I obviously have not gone through pregnancy and childbirth. However, my wife, Amy, who has also been maintaining an approximately one-hundred-pound weight loss in OA, abstained through the birth of our healthy daughter, Elizabeth. Since the credibility of OA stems from firsthand experience (not secondhand advice from those who haven't been there), I think it best to let Amy tell her story in her own words:

> My name is Amy and I am a compulsive overeater. I had been obsessed with food, as well as fat, for most of my life, reaching 239 pounds by the age of twenty-seven. I came into OA not to lose weight, but to achieve sanity around food. The weight loss has been a very pleasant fringe benefit. I was careful not to lose too much weight (or lose it too quickly) because I did not want to lose my period and perhaps endanger my fertility.
>
> Even before I became pregnant, I paid careful attention to the experience of other women in OA who went through pregnancy because I knew that I wanted children someday. By observing how they worked their program around their pregnancies I had a good

idea of what to expect. I knew that it would be a challenge and a struggle to hold onto my abstinence through all of the changes, but I also knew that it was possible because I had seen other women do it. I noticed that the women who successfully abstained through their pregnancies continued to work their program in pretty much the same old way, by going to lots of OA meetings and using the other tools of the program, even though they had to make changes in the way they ate.

Before pregnancy, I had been eating three meals a day and nothing in between. However, during pregnancy it worked better for me to eat several smaller meals each day because of the changes induced by the pregnancy. For one thing, I was nauseous from time to time and found that several smaller meals a day reduced the nausea. A tiny amount of food would make the nausea disappear. My food preferences changed as well, and I found that I could not stand even the smell of certain vegetables.

After having lost so much weight, it felt strange to be gaining weight and accept that as the right thing to do. To develop a belly again was different, to say the least. My weight gain of thirty-eight pounds was within the guidelines set by my midwives. Of course, I still freaked out at the weigh-ins at the midwife's office for fear of gaining too much or too little weight, but I was comforted to know that I was eating right and doing the best I could to take care of my baby. Another weird thing about my pregnancy is that I got no new stretch marks; my skin was so loose as a result of my prior obesity that it did not have to stretch any more.

Since I knew it would be difficult to get to meetings after the birth, I tried to get to as many meetings as I could before the birth. Since the baby was late and the labor long, it was really nice to have the support of the program. OA has taught me to reach out for help when I need it, and that skill has come in handy in many areas of my life, including pregnancy. After the birth, I got back to meetings as soon as possible. An infant is not necessarily too disruptive at a meeting; if Betsy cried I would either nurse her or take her out of the room, but usually she slept.

I continued to eat three meals and two snacks per day. After about three months, I got back to my routine of three meals a day. I did not consciously set out to lose the added weight, but only to continue to abstain from overeating and eat properly for a nursing mother. It took about six months to return to my goal weight, and I think that my long-term breastfeeding accelerated the process.

Abstaining through pregnancy, childbirth, and early motherhood was not easy, but it was worth it. It was one of the best presents I could give my baby or myself, since it meant that my baby and I were getting the right amounts of good nutritious food.

How to prevent cravings

There are different ways to prevent your house from burning down. Once it's on fire, you can use a fire extinguisher to put out small fires before they get out of control. Or you can call the fire department and hope that they can put out the fire. But the best way to prevent your house from burning down is to be careful that fires don't get started in the first place. In other words, don't play with matches, smoke in bed, or keep flammable materials around.

Working the OA program is the best way I know to prevent the cravings for excess food. By using all the tools and working all the Steps, the overwhelming urge to binge goes away. Of course, we all have bad days when we are tempted by food, but for the most part the problem really is removed. It's a long and painstaking process to search out and erase all the old tapes. It doesn't happen overnight. Just as it takes years to learn some skills, it also takes years to learn and practice the OA program as a way of life. What follows are a few more thoughts on things that can be done to prevent the cravings from hitting.

❧ Work with other overeaters
Trying to help other overeaters is the best way to stay sane about food. Of course, if you are already using all the tools and working the Steps, then you are helping other overeaters by going to meetings, doing service, talking to other overeaters on the phone, and sponsoring. Working with other overeaters shows us what works and what doesn't, and gives us a feeling of belonging and fellowship that makes it much easier to get through each day without overeating.

❧ Choose a good food plan
Choosing a sane, well-balanced way of eating helps to prevent food cravings. For newcomers, it may be tempting to try to lose all the weight immediately by starving yourself, but that's a surefire way to produce a lot of cravings. Also, removing any items to which you are sensitive from your food plan will reduce the cravings after the initial withdrawal.

❧ Express gratitude: Count your blessings
One thing I have noticed over the years is that recovering overeaters who are serene and grateful for what they have don't get into overeating; it seems that it is the people who are angry and full of resentment that have trouble. One effective technique for developing a sense of gratitude is to make a list of all the things for which we are grateful. Try writing such a list alphabetically. For example, I am grateful for my Abstinence, my Bicycle, my Car,

and so forth. Usually by the time I get to G or H, I am much less upset about whatever was troubling me.

❦ Deal with your anger

Dealing with anger effectively is essential to holding on to our recovery. When we hold on to all the hurts that have happened to us in our lives and nurture every resentment, we will have no peace. The only thing we will be able to do is to stuff them down with food.

Holding on to resentments hurts us more than the people we resent, since those people are usually unaware that we resent them or don't care if we do. Yet, the resentments within us build up and churn away at our insides. It's no surprise that the Big Book calls resentment the "number one offender."[*]

A good deal of our anger may be justified. We live in an imperfect world where bad things happen. As overeaters, we suffer from a condition most people don't comprehend. When we were fat, we were humiliated, ostracized, and discriminated against because of our looks. Many of us are survivors of crimes and physical and mental abuse.

Justified or not, nursing these grudges won't do us any good. Holding on to every bad thing that has ever been done to us will only hurt us, not help us. When we learn how to deal with our anger, we develop an inner peace and serenity that allows us to deal with an incredible number of unpleasant life circumstances without self-destructing.

So how do we deal with our anger? Dealing with anger doesn't mean bottling it up or letting it fester; it doesn't mean lashing out at everyone whenever we feel bad; it doesn't mean pretending that we're not angry; it doesn't mean rolling over and letting others walk all over us. Dealing with anger means, first of all, identifying that we are angry. We can be so out of touch with our emotions that we don't even know that we are upset. Second, we need to be realistic about the situation. We need to have an accurate assessment of what we can do about it and what we can't. Here is where the Serenity Prayer comes in handy. By realizing that there are some things we can change and some things we can't, we come to terms with the things we can't change.

Next, there has to be the realization that holding on to anger isn't going to do us any good, and that we have to dispose of it properly. One technique for letting go of anger is to write about it. That helps get a lot of the frustration out. For example, "I am mad at my neighbors because their dog keeps messing up my yard and they yell at me when I complain about it. I think that they are insensitive, rude, and selfish."

Prayer is another effective technique for dealing with anger. Ask your

---

[*] *Alcoholics Anonymous*, 64.

Higher Power to take away your anger. It works. Praying for the people you resent is hard, but extremely effective. Try to pray for the people you resent every day, and after a few weeks the resentment will evaporate.

❦ Honesty

Recovery in OA demands that you be rigorously honest with yourself. We have an old saying, "You are as fat as you are dishonest." Our disease taught us how to lie to ourselves, how to justify destructive eating. . . . *One little old bite won't hurt. . . . I earned it. . . . It's organic! . . . I start my diet tomorrow. . . .* These are just some of the excuses we cooked up. We learned to lie to ourselves about how we looked and never really saw ourselves accurately in the mirror. To cover our overeating, many of us were meticulously honest in dealing with others (except around food), but when it came to dealing with ourselves we were as crooked as most of the inmates in the county jail.

One of the most common forms of dishonesty is denial. Many of us refused to admit that we had an eating disorder. We blamed our fat on others. Or we clung to the magical belief that someday our problem would just go away. We thought we could control it and we denied that it bothered us. Despite the fact that my obesity was killing me, my motto was, "If you don't like my weight, that's your problem, not mine!"

Within the program, overeaters fall into denial when they say things like "I don't need to do that." Many of us are reluctant to follow some suggestions of the program, such as taking a personal inventory to examine ourselves thoroughly or stop eating foods that are harmful. Many of us are very self-centered. I always wanted to do things my way or not at all. Unfortunately, doing it my way is what got me into this program. Doing it the program's way is what has given me recovery. We need to be honest with ourselves and accept what we have to do to recover.

We lied to ourselves about what we ate. We thought that if other people didn't see us eat, it didn't count. Some continue this form of self-deception even after joining OA. They claim to be abstaining from overeating and yet they continue to gain weight. Here is a word of warning: if you are lying to yourself, don't expect someone in OA to call you on it. In general, we usually let people figure it out for themselves.

If we continue to practice this type of dishonesty, we will kill ourselves with the consequences of our overeating. Our survival demands that we be honest with ourselves about the nature of our eating disorder and what we are doing to recover from it. We start to practice honesty by talking with other overeaters about what we are eating. For many of us, this is hard; in fact, it was easier to talk about the intimate details of our sex lives than about the foods we were putting into our mouths.

The anonymity of the fellowship is a great help in practicing honesty. Since we frown upon gossip, criticism, and crosstalk, we can be free to talk honestly about whatever we need to talk about without fear that our families and neighbors will find out. At many meetings it's announced, "Who you see here, what you hear here, let it stay here."

Let me add one more word of warning here. Honesty shouldn't be used as an excuse for obnoxiousness and hurting another person's feelings. You can express your feelings honestly and tactfully.

❧ *Go to any lengths*

In determining how much effort to put into recovering from compulsive overeating, you can make two types of errors: (1) you can put too much effort into the program by going to too many meetings and running up your telephone bill, or (2) you can put too little effort into the program by not going to enough meetings, not making enough phone calls, not doing enough service, and eating inappropriately. People who do this often have a low-quality, shaky, white-knuckle abstinence. They run a high risk of returning to compulsive overeating.

This is a serious risk, because for people like us, our lives are on the line. In general, we have to be willing to go as far for our recovery as we did for our disease. Since most of us went to great lengths to get our binge foods, we should be willing to put at least as much time and effort into our recovery.

What to do when the cravings hit

Despite our best plans, there will be times when the food still calls to us. What then? One of the greatest benefits of working the OA program is that, for today, we have been given the ability to choose not to overeat. Previously, that had not been an option. Our addicted brains told us that we had to eat, so we ate.

One thing to remember when we feel like eating is that it's much easier to stay abstinent than it is to get abstinent. Once we start abstaining from overeating, eating sanely becomes a habit with an inertia of its own. After the initial withdrawal passes, we feel good about ourselves and about what we are eating.

But getting started isn't as easy. If you get back into overeating now, you never know how long it will take you to eat sanely again. Many of us thought we could deviate from our food plan because of a trivial special occasion, only to discover that every day yielded another "special occasion." Often it was months, if not years, before we could get back to eating sanely.

As one person said at a meeting, "I know that I have another binge left in me, but I don't know if I have another recovery."

Today, I know that compulsive overeating isn't an option. No matter how difficult life gets, I realize that there is no problem I have that binge-ing my brains out will help. Killing myself with excess food won't fix the dents in my car, nor will it keep me from getting parking tickets if I am ille-gally parked. Compulsive overeating won't make me six feet tall, nor will it make me a millionaire.

By working all the tools and Steps of the OA program, the compulsion to overeat disappears, for the most part. Accepting my eating disorder, doing my best to deal with the emotional damage it caused, and working with others who have my disease have brought me to a point where I no longer crave excess food. The intense cravings to stuff myself with junk food are long gone. Now I consider it a bad day if I start counting the hours until my next meal.

My own experience in the program has shown me that the cravings will go away if I don't act on them. In other words, I won't die if I don't take that first compulsive bite. Furthermore, I will feel a lot better in the long run because I know that I am taking good care of myself. Remember the phrase "This too shall pass." It includes cravings to overeat. A friend of mine in OA once decided to time how long it took one of his cravings to pass. It passed eighteen minutes later! Be aware that the cravings may hit with a one-two punch; they may be intense one moment and then go away. We breathe a sigh of relief and then, wham! they come back.

Still, the question remains, What do I do when the craving hits? Fortu-nately, this program has given us a bag of tools and techniques to get through difficult situations. Not all of them are feasible for everyone every time, but all of them come in handy at one time or another.

❧ Make a phone call

Phone calls are cheap; even long-distance calls are cheaper than the costs of compulsive overeating. Picking up the phone is a good way to avoid pick-ing up food. Talking to another compulsive overeater often helps us to get through those difficult situations. We don't even have to admit that we're feeling the urge to eat, but admitting it often makes it go away.

❧ Read some literature

OA publishes an inexpensive pamphlet called *Before You Take That First Compulsive Bite, Remember . . .* that is quite helpful in rough situations. It's small enough to carry around and cheap enough to keep extra copies in the car and at work. The AA book *Living Sober* also has wonderful advice in it to help you get through rough periods.

❦ *Drink something*

Sometimes, as crazy as it may seem, we mistake thirst for hunger. Drinking a glass or two of water or some other liquid will make the "hungry growlies" go away. I find this is especially helpful when I am attending a social occasion where food is available in abundance; when I see other people putting things in their mouths, I want to put something in mine. Noncaloric liquids help.

❦ *Take a walk*

Light physical activity is a great mood elevator and can often take cravings away. Many times we may feel a restless energy that we think is hunger. Actually, it's our bodies telling us to get more activity; in the past, the food silenced this message from our bodies and took that energy away.

❦ *Distract yourself*

Getting involved in an activity that takes attention away from our problems is an excellent way to forget about food. This is one of the reasons why working with others is stressed so much in the OA program. When we get involved with others, we tend to forget our own problems.

❦ *Get to an OA meeting*

At an OA meeting, you will meet other overeaters who are trying to recover, and you may hear just what you need to hear. At the very least, it will keep you away from the refrigerator for a while.

❦ *Pray*

Don't laugh or sneer if you haven't tried it. You don't have to pay to do it, and you don't even have to tell anyone you're doing it. You don't even have to believe in a god. The Serenity Prayer often helps, although when times get rough my favorite prayer is "God, take it away! Please!" It may be a crutch, but it's better to walk with crutches than to crawl in misery.

❦ *Do a mini-inventory*

There are often logical reasons why we crave excess food. Part of having an eating disorder means that our bodies misinterpret many signals as a need for food. For example, some people are sensitive to certain foods, which may set off a desire to overeat. In other people, strong emotions, such as anger, can set off the urge to eat. These cravings can be indistinguishable from real hunger.

The quickest form of a mini-inventory is to think of the slogan HALT: Don't get too Hungry, Angry, Lonely, or Tired. These states often make our judgment questionable. If we find ourselves in one of these conditions, we had better be aware that what seems like legitimate hunger may be a misinterpretation of other feelings.

One way to do a more thorough mini-inventory is to do a mental Tenth Step before you fall asleep. Since this disease is physical, emotional, and spiritual, ask yourself a set of questions to see if you can unearth the reasons for the craving:

- *Where am I physically?* Am I getting enough rest and exercise? Is there anything in my food plan that may be setting off a craving for more food?
- *Where am I emotionally?* Am I angry or upset with anyone? Am I afraid or worried about something? Am I dealing with the main issues in my life?
- *Where am I spiritually?* Did I remember to pray and meditate? How am I working my program? Am I remembering to reach out to others? Am I working all the tools of the program?

This mini-inventory will often help to unearth the reasons for food cravings. It may or may not be an accurate explanation, but it often helps the cravings dissipate and points out actions we can take to avoid having them in the future.

Losing the weight

As we continue to abstain from overeating, an amazing thing happens to those of us who are overweight—we begin to lose weight. (However, none of us ever really "loses" the weight, since we all know exactly where to find it.)

Let me suggest that shedding pounds is actually the easy part; not overeating is the hard part. When your body takes in fewer calories than it burns up, it will automatically lose weight. Many of us cherished the notion that our metabolism was so efficient that we were doomed to be fat. Indeed, some of us have trained our bodies, through years of starvation diets, to be very efficient in holding on to calories. But the laws of thermodynamics haven't been repealed: if we want to take off pounds, we need to consume fewer calories than we burn. In other words, eat less and exercise more.

Here is my experience. I got an OA sponsor that I could work with every day. As I mentioned earlier, she suggested that I make ninety OA meetings in ninety days. I got abstinent on a rather loosely defined food plan of my own design: three meals a day, no junk, all four food groups, small portions. It was very rough for the first couple of days, since I was going through physical withdrawal from the junk food I had been eating. I was tired and irritable, and the cravings were intense at times.

As I started going to lots of OA meetings, I began to find out what other recovering overeaters ate. Some of the people who had taken off, and kept off, large amounts of weight revealed that not only did they have problems with sugar, but also with some other high-carbohydrate foods, such as bread. It seemed that certain foods set off a craving in them for more food.

At this point, I was really desperate. I was abstaining, but just barely hanging on because the cravings were intense. I knew that I couldn't last long the way I was going. As an experiment, I thought I would try to follow what seemed to be working for others like me, so I stopped eating the heavy starchy foods. Over the next few days, the cravings to overeat diminished rapidly. Why? I don't know. Whether my reactions to certain foods are based on the neurotransmitters in my brain or on the way I was fed by my parents is something I will probably never untangle. I could come up with dozens of plausible explanations, but for now I just accept my own experience and learn from it.

The weight started coming off rapidly. I sensed that the people at the OA meetings knew what they were talking about and could help me to keep the weight off as well as lose it, so I continued to go to meetings and became actively involved in OA. I started doing service jobs, such as setting up the literature for a meeting, because they told me that the pounds would come off faster if I did service. I continued to read the OA literature and started to read the book *Alcoholics Anonymous*. I weighed myself only once a month because that's what was suggested. I started to work the Steps of the program because I noticed that the people who maintained their weight loss all said that they had worked them.

It took me about ten months for OA to take off approximately 110 pounds, a reduction that I have maintained (plus or minus five pounds) for over a decade.[*] But adjusting to the changes that take place *after* weight reduction has taken years. (I will talk more about maintenance later; that's just one of the stages we go through as we get better.) The next section talks about each of these stages in more detail.

The stages of recovery

It takes time for most things in life to happen, including recovery. We go through a lot of predictable stages as we recover, and as the saying goes, "Forewarned is forearmed." So by becoming aware of these stages, we'll find it easier to deal with them.

---

[*]My weight reduction was more rapid than it is for most OA members. For some, losing weight this fast could be hazardous. Make sure you get good medical advice when losing weight.

❧ *Withdrawal*

When we go from bingeing on thousands of calories a day to eating moderately, our body fights back. Let's face it. If the sudden cessation of overeating instantly made us feel great, we would have done it a long time ago without OA. We can expect to feel tired and irritable and to experience cravings, but the worst of the withdrawal is over after a week or two.

For newcomers, withdrawal may be masked by a honeymoon abstinence, sometimes called the "pink cloud" stage. Crawling through the doors of OA for the first time, most of us are truly desperate and are willing to go to any lengths to recover. When we discover the fellowship and start working the program, abstinence seems to follow almost effortlessly. As a matter of fact, it may become so easy that newcomers are tempted to skimp on the rest of the program, such as making phone calls or working the Steps. So easy, in fact, that taking the first bite doesn't seem that bad. The food lies to us and tells us that we can now control it whenever we want, just by going to meetings, so it's okay to start overeating. It's the old diet mentality of "I'll eat today and diet tomorrow." Unfortunately, it's usually much harder to get abstinent the second time around. As is said at meetings, "It's a lot easier to stay on than to get on."

❧ *The "Screw it" stage*

After about two weeks, expect a brief but sudden period of temptation. That old "Screw it!" feeling may hit. If you don't act on it, it will pass as quickly as it comes. By about three weeks you may notice that your clothes will start feeling looser. That's a wonderful feeling.

Your recovery will pick up momentum in the weeks ahead. As you go to more and more meetings, read the literature, and start working the Steps, things seem to fall into place. The pounds start to roll off.

❧ *Remembering only the good times*

After several months of abstinence, perhaps about five months, a period of craziness seems to hit. This seems to be a common experience not just for recovering overeaters, but for people recovering from other addictions as well. The memories of the pain caused by overeating fade, but the memories of the good times we had with food come back. We may forget to call others in the program, and our spiritual contact may go out the window. The cravings may come back. They will pass if we don't eat.

❧ *The first anniversary*

Emotional jitters can arise around program milestones, such as abstinence anniversaries. You may fear that somehow you will mess up just before your anniversary. The first anniversary of getting abstinent is often the hardest.

There may be a sense of unreality to it, as if you can't believe it. It feels like something has to go wrong. Fear of success may creep in. The old low self-esteem may kick in and say that you don't really deserve it. There is also a sense that this new way of life is becoming real, that it's not just a dream or a temporary diet, and this can be scary.

The sailing then gets pretty smooth, but there will be occasional storms. We aren't cured. All we get is a daily reprieve from our eating disorder. I have met many people who forgot this; they started to slack off in their meeting attendance and relapsed after years of abstinence.

℣ The second year

Around our second year of recovery some of us go through the "terrible twos." We may become obnoxious OA know-it-alls, inflicting our opinions on one and all, whether they want them or not. This stage fades away as we develop more experience and maturity in our recovery.

It's sometimes said that in the first year of recovery we tend to focus on the physical side of our disease; in the second year, the emotional; and in the third year, the spiritual. I don't think it breaks down quite so neatly, but the ordering is roughly accurate. Since it's hard to grow emotionally or spiritually while fogged out on food, and since most newcomers are anxious for physical recovery, most start there. Dealing with the physical side requires a great deal of attention as we wrestle with the issues of how, what, and when to eat. Then, as we put down the food, the emotional damage becomes apparent and demands attention. Finally, we realize that we must further our spiritual development if we are going to hold on to our physical and emotional recovery.

Some of the predictable phases, such as abstinence anniversary jitters, are related to time; others are related to weight. Dropping below the two-hundred-pound mark or fitting into certain sizes of clothes can cause mixed feelings. We are often joyful at the achievement but saddened that the rush of excitement we get doesn't last as long as we would like. A friend of mine says that no one was ever as thin as he was when the scale hit 299 on the way down. Getting halfway to a goal causes fear for some of us because that's when we would slack off in our dieting days. (Reaching goal weight is a milestone that deserves a whole section of its own. See page 123.)

℣ Other stages

We may pass through other stages in recovery that aren't associated with the calendar or the scale. Many of us go through a mourning period in which we mourn the loss of food. Even though the food hurt us severely, we still had a lot of good times with it. Brief periods of sadness at various times during the first year or two of abstinence are par for the course. Don't beat yourself up when they hit. Just remember that they will pass and that overeating won't solve any of your problems.

The martyr stage. Some of us go through a martyr period when our pride gets out of line. We expect the whole world to applaud because we have stopped killing ourselves. We can be a real pain to be around in this stage, but eventually it too passes.

Fear and rigidity. After decades of struggling with food, when we finally find something that works we cling to it with all our might, the way a drowning person clings to a life preserver. We may become afraid that if we make any changes in our program, we will return to the compulsive hell from which we narrowly escaped. We may not want to hear about people who are trying to work OA a different way, or from those who are using a different food plan. We may be afraid that they will lead us astray. We may become especially fearful of hearing about other people's problems with food for fear that they may rub off on us. But we can relax. As long as we continue to perform the actions that we see working for other overeaters, we will get better.

I take a Darwinian view of OA. When a lot of people try many different things, we gain much experience quickly about what does and doesn't work. The practices that work will stick around in a "survival of the fittest" manner, and those that don't work will fade away. Thus, we need not be afraid to hear about how other people are eating differently than we are, or about the trouble they are having with food, because we can learn from their experience.

The crutch stage. Many of us go through a crutch stage in our first few years when we use large amounts of diet soda, coffee, or sugarless gum. We manage to switch our addiction from the fattening binge foods that were killing us to low-calorie substitutes. It can be frightening to realize that we are still addicts and are still practicing our addiction. When I was chewing five packs of sugarless gum each day, I got diarrhea and gas from all the sorbitol it contains. My jaw was sore from all the chewing, yet I couldn't seem to get enough. Drinking thirty cups of decaffeinated coffee in a day resulted in frequent trips to the bathroom. Fortunately, I got tired of my chemical crutches and eventually learned to live without them. In the meantime, remember that it's better to drink a lot of diet soda than to carry around a hundred extra pounds. Try not to worry too much about it.

Food dreams. It's quite common to have occasional food dreams even years after we stop overeating. I have heard that those who have quit smoking or drinking have similar dreams. Food dreams are frightening because they are often so vivid and seem so real. Whenever I have one, I expect to find candy wrappers all over the house when I wake up. Since I am not an expert on dreams, I will leave the interpretations to the professionals, but such dreams don't appear to be cause for alarm. It seems that mainly abstinent people get them. I find that talking about them with other overeaters helps to make the fear and the guilt they bring up fade quickly.

The staleness stage. From time to time we all go through a period of staleness. We are bored by just about everything. It seems as if meetings are the same old stuff, and we wonder why we are making phone calls, because we say the same old things. Even our food starts to taste boring. Fortunately, these stale periods do pass and there are ways to make them pass more quickly. If the meetings that you are going to seem stale, try some different OA meetings. Instead of calling your OA cronies, call some people that you don't normally talk to. And try talking to others in the program about what they eat—you are bound to get lots of interesting ideas for some new abstinent meals.

It's common at times to dislike being in the program. It sometimes seems like too much of a burden to go to meetings. We may grow tired of the routines and the discipline that we have established. We may want to isolate ourselves. Fortunately, these periods pass as well. One good way to ensure that they pass without overeating is to have some service commitments that get you to meetings when you don't want to go. Sponsoring people also ensures that you get some phone calls even when you don't want to make phone calls yourself.

Relapse. Unfortunately, many of us pass through a relapse stage. Our disease isn't only cunning, baffling, and powerful, it's also patient. Relapse is a frightening and painful part of our disease, and the threat of it is always there. It's a topic that demands a section of its own. (See page 136.) But relapse isn't inevitable, and everyone who keeps coming to meetings gets back on track sooner or later.

As a result of using the tools and working the Steps, we are delivered from the compulsion to binge our brains out. But the compulsion can also hit us again. The OA program is designed to give us the lifestyle we need to prevent the cravings from hitting as much as possible, and to keep us from eating when they do.

The food will call again, even if only in a gentle whisper. When this happens, I am reminded of the coastal fog that hangs just off the shore of San Francisco. There are times when the weather is sunny for a long time and I think it will never end. There are other times when the fog seems never-ending and I think I'll never see the sun again. There are also days when I can see the fog hanging off the coast, just waiting for the right winds to push it my way. Food is the same way. Most of the time it's off my back, and it seems like it will never be a problem again. Other days, it seems as if it's all I can do to get from one meal to the next. But it does pass, just like the fog.

Handling the emotional storm

Many of us stuffed all our feelings with food, the good and the bad, and now we have to live without this narcotic. When we put the food down, a lot of unfamiliar feelings come up. Most of us were so numb from our eating excesses that we were not aware of many normal, everyday feelings. But as the numbness wears off, we again feel the emotions that other people feel. This can be scary and can tempt us to overeat. But overeating won't make our lives any better. It won't solve any of our problems and in fact will create new ones. Today, we can feel our feelings, both the painful and the pleasurable ones.

It's tempting to think that no one could possibly understand what we are going through. Our terminal uniqueness told us that we were different from everyone else and that what applied to others didn't apply to us. We sometimes felt that we were both worse and better than everyone else at the same time. Even though we are individuals, we overeaters have many things in common when it comes to feelings. This section describes how we can deal with them without overeating.

❦ *Dealing with fear*

We have suffered a lot from fear. We were afraid of what other people thought of us because we were fat. Or when we were thin, we were terrified of getting fat again. We feared that we wouldn't fit into restaurant booths, we feared that we wouldn't get enough food, we feared not fitting into our clothes. At times, we feared that we would never wake up again; other times, we feared that we would wake up again. Many of us were paralyzed by our fears and prevented from living a full life.

We were afraid of accepting our eating disorder, because then we would have to do something about it. We feared humiliation when others found out about our eating disorder. As if they didn't already know by looking at us? Even purgers are surprised to find out how many people knew of or suspected their purging long before they were told. But our friends, co-workers, and families have known us for a long time. They have watched our diets, binges, and fasts. They have seen us lose massive amounts of weight and gain it back again. They know we have a problem with food, even though some of them assured us that we didn't.

Fear of failure plagued many of us when we came into OA. We had tried so many schemes before that had not worked, and we were afraid that OA might be just another false hope. We were afraid of public humiliation if we were to lose weight again and then gain it all back still another time. Some of us were afraid that we were such hopeless cases that not even OA would work for us. But we were pleasantly surprised to learn that OA has a high success rate for those who stick with it. An old program saying goes, "There are no failures in OA, only slow successes."

Fear of the unknown. Fear often comes up when we put down the food. Much of it is fear of the unknown. We've spent our lives developing our old way of living, but it stopped working. We've had a lot of experience in being self-centered and leaning on food as a crutch to get us through. When we let go of the food, we wonder what will replace it. *How will I survive when they pass the doughnuts at the Monday staff meeting? How could I possibly live without my food? What will become of me? Will I turn into one of those diet-and-exercise fanatics I always detested? Will I turn into a Holy Roller or some New Age space case?* When we try something new there is the fear of what might or might not happen.

Some of us were afraid of having to deal with physical or emotional pain without the narcotic of food. Even though the consequences of our overeating were severe, the momentary pleasure that food gave us was real, even if it was not worth the price we had to pay for it.

What do you do when painful feelings bring up thoughts of food? The best advice given to me was just to let it hurt. Whatever we are feeling may be painful, but harming ourselves with too much food or harmful food won't make our lives any better. Overeating will only temporarily distract us from the problem by creating an even bigger problem. By numbing ourselves with food, all we do is neglect our problems so that they fester and get worse. All the feelings we have stuffed down with food have to be dealt with sooner or later, and the longer we wait, the harder it gets.

Fear in relationships. We may fear recovery because we don't know how it will affect our relationships. When we were overeating, our families, friends, and co-workers knew what to expect of us. But when we suddenly embark on a program of personal growth, they may become confused and not know what to expect. Some of those around us have their own food, alcohol, or other drug problems, and they may feel threatened when we start to recover. Or we may fear that they will abandon us as we get well.

Many of us fear intimate relationships. Our emotional development was retarded by our addiction to overeating. Food was an abusive lover that we dared not leave despite the suffering it caused us. While others were learning how to interact with people, we were learning how to hide our binges. We lacked the social skills we needed to establish and maintain relationships. Many of us have come from dysfunctional families that presented poor models for healthy relationships. The only relationships we had were often less than satisfactory, so we became afraid that as we lost weight we would find ourselves in other harmful relationships.

Fear of switching addictions. Because we are addicted in one area of our lives, we are vulnerable to becoming addicted in other areas. Some of us are afraid that we will become compulsive about sex or spending as a substitute for food. Some are even afraid of developing an addiction to, or at least an unhealthy dependence on, OA. But Twelve Step programs are designed to break our addictive patterns so that we don't have to live life as practicing addicts. Even if we temporarily switch compulsions to a less harmful one, such as sugarless gum, we are still making progress.

Fear of being thin. One fear that has probably been blown out of proportion by some well-meaning pop therapists is the fear of being thin. For them, it provides a handy excuse for why fat people are fat, but one that doesn't hold water. Fearing being thin inaccurately describes our feelings. Overeaters usually have little fear about having a normal body size. We may fear the loss of our excuses for why our lives haven't lived up to our fantasies. We may be afraid of intimate relationships, or that we will become promiscuous. We may be unable to let go of the distorted belief that body size is the same as power. But we usually have little fear about having a thin body.

So what do we do about these fears? Reviewing them thoroughly as part of our Step Four personal inventory helps. Finding out what we fear and why is one of the first steps in dealing with them. Talking about them with others in the program, many of whom have had the same fears, is a tremendous help. It may sound hokey, but turning them over to God in prayer also does wonders for our peace of mind.

❦ Self-pity

Self-pity is an emotion that can poison us from within and make us more susceptible to getting back into overeating. There is an old AA saying: "Poor me. Poor me. Pour me a drink."

Most of us have things to feel sorry about. But wallowing in self-pity does us no good. We can't do anything to change the past. I have observed many people in OA who whined at meetings for months and years and never seemed to get better, physically or emotionally. As an old-timer said at an OA meeting, "If your parents put you on the toilet backward when you were six months old, shame on them. If, thirty years later, you are still sitting backwards, shame on you."

One of the beautiful things about OA is that we don't have to be victims any more. Yes, some things may have happened to us, but we learn how to put them behind us, to carry on and live life to its fullest potential.

❦ Depression

Overeaters tend to suffer from depression at higher rates than the general population. Far from being the typical blues that everyone gets from time to time, some types of depression can last for months. Loss of appetite is a classic symptom of depression, although in overeaters the opposite can occur. Many of us attempted to medicate ourselves with food to improve our moods, only to find out that the food was a rip-off high. Any mood improvements were short-lived and followed by even deeper feelings of hopelessness.

Many of us found that our depression cleared up when we began to eat properly. Most of the lethargy left when we got the junk food—especially sugar, alcohol, and refined starches—out of our systems. Exercise also helped to improve our moods.

The consensus among professionals today is that much severe depression is biochemically based, although the exact mechanism that causes it isn't clear. Great advances have been made in treating depression with antidepressant medications. If you suffer from severe depression and your doctor prescribes medication, it will probably help you. But be warned that one of the side effects of some common antidepressants includes a strong increase in appetite and a feeling of nausea if you don't eat. This means that you will be tempted to eat more, and if you eat more you will gain weight. If you get hit with this side effect, talk to your doctor and pharmacist to see if they can prescribe an alternative medication or therapy.

❦ Loving yourself and dealing with self-hatred

Self-hatred has scarred many an overeater. We have been ostracized for a long time because of our fat, and many of us have internalized this. We blamed ourselves for having an eating disorder and hated ourselves for our weakness. Many of us learned self-hatred from our messed-up families. Some of us read psychobabble that said self-hatred is the cause of obesity. Whether self-hatred is the cause or the effect of our eating disorder is irrelevant. What matters is that we have it and need to deal with it.

Taking care of ourselves is one of the most effective ways of learning to love ourselves. By acting as if we love ourselves, sooner or later we actually do. By giving ourselves the right amount of food—not too much and not too little—we show that we really care about ourselves. We don't harm ourselves with junk food, and we don't skimp on quality anymore. We are worth it. As I heard one overeater say, "I figure if I am only going to eat four ounces of meat at dinner, then I am going to eat four ounces of the best meat I can find."

For some of us, self-hatred may stem from guilt we have about events that happened long ago. Often, just talking about the events with a sympathetic person can diminish the guilt and the pain. This is one of the reasons we stress a personal inventory as a part of Step Four. By taking a good hard look at ourselves, we expose many of the things that cause us problems. Even though they may be distressing to us, they are often no big deal in the grand scheme of things. Usually, there is nothing we can do about the past anyway. Talking about these things with another human being as a part of Step Five provides a way to get rid of the guilt and pain and then get on with our lives.

❧ Growing up and dealing with our inner child

Most of us overeaters suffered from a general lack of maturity, not only concerning food, but also in other areas of our lives. We clung to magical thinking; we thought that food wouldn't make us fat, as long as no one saw us eating it. We thought that all of our problems would disappear the day that we hit our goal weight.

Yet, many of us were denied part of our childhood and thrust prematurely into adulthood. For example, our large size forced us to shop for clothes in the adult section when we were still children. Some of us were forced to care for ourselves and our brothers and sisters because our parents were unable to, so we missed the carefree part of growing up.

It's easy to get caught up in self-pity over these things and to wallow in childishness because of them. Some of us abuse the unconditional acceptance in OA and stay immature. Some OA members talk about having to listen to their child within. When this means getting in touch with the part of ourselves that's hopeful and trusting and eager to learn how to live, that's good. But when this means being unwilling to take responsibility for impulsive behavior or hanging on to self-pity and old resentments, that's unhealthy.

We all know what immature kids want: candy, and lots of it. If we start listening to the immature part of ourselves within, we shouldn't be surprised if it screams for candy.

❧ Family issues

Few of us come from a family that's totally well. Many of our family members are also overeaters. Alcoholism and other drug abuse are common in overeaters' families. There may have been physical and emotional abuse. Yet there may also have been a lot of love and affection; thus we may have mixed feelings about our families. Some family members are our staunchest supporters as well as our severest critics, and they can send us into emotional gyrations with little effort.

Don't be surprised if strong feelings about your family come up after you stop overeating. We were often so emotionally numb from overeating that we were unable to sort out the kinds of things that most people sort out as part of becoming adults. Consequently, we may have a lot of catching up to do. There may be long-standing resentments that need to be dealt with. Fortunately, OA offers several proven tools to deal with our feelings of anger and resentment.

In addition to dealing with resentments from the past, we also need to deal with the changing relationships of the present. People don't stay the same forever, and neither do families. When one member changes, the other members change as well. Thus, when you start to recover, there are bound to be some changes in your relationship with your family. Most of the changes will be positive. Those who truly love you will want you to take care of yourself and will support you. Those who love you have also shared your pain, even if you were so numb that you couldn't tell they cared. You will find that you can communicate with them in ways that were not possible before, and there may be greater sharing than you ever thought possible.

On the other hand, some family members may feel threatened by your getting better, especially if they are practicing overeaters themselves. They may fear the loss of a binge buddy or resent the attention that you are getting.

Other family members just won't understand. They will question why you are going to so many meetings and why you haven't been cured yet. They may confuse your recovery with some weird diet you once tried. Be patient. You need not explain everything to them all at once or convince them that this time you have found the answer. All you need to do is to continue to abstain from overeating and work the rest of the OA program and you will figure out how to live with your family members one day at a time without self-destructing.

If you have problems that stem from the addictions of others, whether they are in your family or not, you should check out groups such as Al-Anon and Adult Children of Alcoholics (ACA). But don't expect those programs to do anything for your overeating. It's tempting to think that since such programs are similar to OA, that they will do the same things. They don't. You have to work with other overeaters to get better from overeating, and that's why we have separate Anonymous programs for separate problems.

❦ Making changes slowly

We go through many changes as we recover from the damage done by our disease. Our judgment was warped by years of food abuse, and it takes time to sort out how to live without excess food. For this reason, it's usually recommended that we go slowly when making major changes in our lives.

We may get extremely enthusiastic about taking care of ourselves. For the first time in our lives, it seems as if our food problem has been solved. Now, what other problems in our lives are we going to fix? We may be tempted to make many major changes all at once—perhaps it's time to get a new job, find a spouse, go back to school, move to a new place. But remember that the disease is cunning, baffling, and powerful. It can be arrested, one day at a time, by working the OA program, but it can't be cured. If we let other matters divert our attention from recovery, then we are in grave danger of returning to overeating.

Any major life change can bring up intense feelings that we are inexperienced in handling. A case in point is my cross-country move. I had tried several geographic cures over the years, thinking that a new opportunity in a new place would allow me to live happily ever after. It was easy; I just packed up and moved. Unfortunately, I usually discovered that I had brought all my problems, including my eating disorder, with me. But because I was in a constant food fog that numbed my feelings, the fact that I was leaving my friends and family never bothered me. After all, candy bars are available almost everywhere, and I thought they were my only true friends. Then, after two years in OA, I moved three thousand miles to take advantage of a great educational opportunity, and I was amazed at the feelings that came up when I realized I was going to miss many of my friends. Although I had moved several times before, all of those moves had been "sugar-coated," so I had never felt the pain of parting.

It's not wise to tempt fate early in recovery. Since it takes quite a while to assimilate all that the OA program has to offer, it's wise to be patient and cautious in making any major life changes in your first year of recovery.

About relationships and recovery

Years of ostracism and humiliation from a society that worships thinness have warped the way we relate to others, and this damage takes time to repair. Not only were we shunned because of our obesity, but we also pushed people away so that we could practice our addiction. "Normal" people just couldn't understand the way we ate. Many of us were so afraid of rejection that we rejected others before they could reject us.

❦ *Out of isolation*

Because of this isolation, many of us lacked the skills needed to find and maintain healthy relationships—not just intimate relationships, but plain old friendships. Many healthy people don't like to be around practicing addicts because practicing addicts tend to be manipulative, self-centered people who really don't care about others. Some of our old friendships were based on food and substance abuse, and these so-called friends lost interest in us when they could no longer use us for their purposes.

For me, the isolation extended back to my youth. Compulsive overeating deprived me of a normal adolescence. When my peers were going through the experiences of maturing and learning to relate to other people, I was alone and feeding my face. I avoided socializing and participating in sports because I was embarrassed at being fat and awkward. Fear of others' comments turned the simple act of changing my clothes in the locker room into a trauma. Overeating shut me off from the activities of normal kids, and being shut off from the activities of normal kids made me overeat. It was a vicious circle. I spent the rest of my time reading, listening to heavy metal music, and hiding in the darkroom where I developed photographs— hardly activities where one learns how to relate to others. After I lost the weight, I discovered that I had no idea of how the dating game was played; I ended up going through my teens when I was in my twenties.

Those who were not obese as children may not have my particular emotional scars, although they have their own. Many overeaters have felt isolated because "normal" people can't understand our compulsion. The shame about our secret and the fear that it would be discovered have left their mark on us.

It takes time to learn how to have healthy relationships. Just realizing the extent of the damage is a good start. Attending OA meetings allows us to end the isolation and be with other people. Calling OA members gives us much-needed practice in reaching out. As we develop more self-confidence, others will sense this and want to be around us more.

☙ *Jumping the gun*

After years of isolation, it's tempting to make up for lost time and seek intimate relationships quickly. But the best advice is to take it slowly at first. As a matter of fact, the OA pamphlet *Now that You've Reached Goal Weight, Now What?* recommends that you don't even think about having a serious relationship until you have maintained goal weight for a year.

When I first heard this advice from some male old-timers, I thought they were just being selfish. Of course, I ignored them. But my observations and experiences over the years have shown me the wisdom of their advice. First of all, it's too easy to get involved with the wrong person. Our overwhelming loneliness may lead us to grab on to the first person who will have us, whether or not that person is right for us. Remember that two sick people don't make a healthy relationship. Such a relationship must end sooner or later if we are to maintain our sanity. And the intense feelings that come up as a relationship falters are very difficult to deal with, especially if we have never dealt with them before.

Another reason to avoid a serious relationship for the first year is that you are changing rapidly. Even if you found the person who was absolutely perfect for you today, you will be such a different person tomorrow that it would not be fair to you or to the person to get serious too fast. Many times we have chosen partners who actively encouraged our disease. I know a woman in the program who got involved with a man who was not in OA but who had a fetish for severely obese women. When her weight fell below two hundred pounds, he was no longer interested in her and she was heartbroken.

❦ Remain committed to OA

An additional danger is that a relationship can devour the time that you must devote to your recovery. I have seen many people, both men and women, come to OA and immediately lose a lot of weight. Then their social life picks up and their meeting attendance drops. Here is where the food is at its most deceptive, because their eating remains appropriate for a while. But eventually the lack of OA meetings takes its toll and they end up overeating again.

It's very tempting to get romantically involved with someone in the OA program. After years of loneliness, it was wonderful for me to discover that there was a whole fellowship of people like me who spoke my language. Here were a bunch of people who knew what I was like and liked me anyway. It was a great relief to be accepted at last as one of the crowd, even though the crowd knew the crazy things I had done with food. It seemed like a natural place to look for a serious relationship.

❦ Pitfalls of OA romance

But intimate relationships within OA present their own difficulties. You may become involved with someone who isn't right for you. If the relationship ends, it may be painfully awkward to see him or her at meetings. This can tempt you to stop going to meetings, which is one of the worst things that a recovering compulsive overeater can do.

A lapse in meeting attendance is usually the first sign of an impending relapse. If you are in a city that has many OA meetings to choose from, it may be possible to go to different meetings. But in areas without many meetings, this isn't possible. Let nothing stop you from going to the meetings you need to recover. It may feel awkward to see men or women you used to date, but you will get over it. Fortunately, this program teaches us how to deal with others. By doing the self-assessment and inventory in Steps Four and Ten and making amends where needed, you will learn how to live and deal with others.

But don't let me scare you away from the right relationship when the time is appropriate. I have known many people who have had very meaningful and fulfilling relationships with others in the program, several of which resulted in happy marriages. I met my wife in OA. The important thing to ask yourself before you get involved with a program person is, *How will I feel when I run into him or her at meetings if it doesn't work out? How will I feel if he or she stops seeing me and starts dating someone else and I run into both of them at a meeting?*

For those who are unskilled in relationships, as I was, keep this in mind: when you do start searching for a relationship, expect your heart to be broken many times. It would be extremely rare if the first person you met turned out to be your lifetime partner. As the old saying goes, you have to kiss a lot of toads before you find your prince. Also, be careful! You may feel a strong temptation to make up for lost time as you start enjoying your new, thinner body. Find out about and then practice safe sexual behavior. Don't let a sexually transmitted disease take the fun out your recovery.

Spirituality, or What's this God stuff?

OA isn't a religious program, but a spiritual one. We have found that several spiritual tools are useful for recovering from our food addiction. We start and end meetings with simple prayers, and people will use words like "God," "meditation," and "prayer."

This can be a real turnoff for some. Many of us were suspicious at first that OA might be some kind of cult. Fortunately, we relaxed once we discovered that we didn't have to join any church, leave our present one, or follow any guru in order to get better.

It's okay to have lots of doubts and resistance about the spiritual side of OA. Just try to keep an open mind and don't knock it if you haven't tried it. Most of us had reservations about it when we came into the program. The reason for OA's spiritual side is that our experience shows that it works. Most OA members find over the years that a spiritual path will help them with further spiritual development. As one OA member put it, "OA won't open the gates of Heaven to let you in, but it will open the gates of Hell to let you out."

✻ *Pick the Higher Power of your choice*
One spiritual tool that we find useful is believing in a "Power greater than ourselves," which some call God and others call Higher Power. In other words, we realize that we don't run the universe all by ourselves. Most of us already had such a power, and it was food. No matter how hard we tried, the food had power over us. What we need is a Power greater than the next bite.

We don't have to believe in anyone else's concept of God, and certainly not in the concept of some punishing deity that we may have picked up in childhood. God isn't the bogeyman. We are free to choose our own conception of God, because if God can appear any way God wants, God can appear as anything we can possibly conceive. We don't have to figure out the answers to all the great questions about the nature of the universe. As I once heard at a meeting, "The only thing you need to know about God is that you aren't God." Although the Steps refer to God as "Him," your Higher Power doesn't have to be a "Him." This was just common usage when the Steps were first written in the 1930s. There is now an active movement within OA to substitute *God* for *Him* in the Steps. But it will probably take a long time before this happens because of the cumbersome nature of OA's group-conscience decision making.

Many who have problems with the idea of a Higher Power use the OA group as a Higher Power. With over 150,000 overeaters around the world, OA has a lot more experience with recovery than any one of us can learn in a lifetime. That's certainly a Power greater than any of us individually.

❦ *The power of prayer*

Prayer is another spiritual tool that's incredibly useful. Many of us, as practicing addicts, found that we were so stoned on food that we couldn't have any kind of conscious contact with God. But prayer helps us to turn our focus away from a self-centered existence, and as we turn our problems and troubles over to our Higher Power, we find it easier to deal with them.

If you are having trouble praying, just remember that you don't have to believe in God to pray. It still works anyway. I know an atheist who thinks that all prayer does is play around with the alpha waves in his brain, but he still prays to a God he doesn't want to believe in because he benefits from it.

Few of us understand how a television works. We just plug it in, turn it on, and pay attention. We don't have to know how or why prayer works either. All we have to do is do it. We don't have to pay anybody anything to pray. We don't need an advanced degree in theology to do it. We don't even have to tell anyone that we are doing it. We have nothing to lose from prayer. It costs nothing and can provide great benefits, so we use it.

❦ *Meditating to listen*

Meditation is another powerful spiritual tool that adds greatly to the quality of our life. I have heard it said that prayer is talking to God and meditation is listening. My serenity and peace of mind are much greater on days when I meditate than on days when I don't.

There are different ways to meditate, just as there are different ways to pray. Try talking to others in the program or to a priest, minister, rabbi, or other spiritual guide. (For specific meditation techniques, see the discussion of Step Eleven on page 115.)

❦ *Spiritual dawn*

You will also hear the terms "spiritual experience" and "spiritual awakening" in the program. As the result of working the OA program, many of us "wake up" spiritually. I like to think of spiritual awakening in terms of waking up from a very deep sleep. Some of us wake up quickly when an alarm goes off; others wake up slowly with a gradual awareness of the dawn. Indeed, some of us are still groggy long after we wake up. For me, this means that I went from being a spiritually numb and self-centered person to one who is aware that he isn't the center of the universe. I am aware that God is out there, and it does me good to try to talk to God.

If you are having trouble with the spiritual side of OA, don't let your reservations stop you from getting what you can out of the rest of the OA program. There are plenty of other benefits. If you try the spiritual side and are still having problems, try praying for willingness and you will get some.

The AA and OA literature provides a great deal of guidance for those who have had problems with some of the spiritual principles of the program, as most of us have. The AA Big Book has a powerful chapter entitled "We Agnostics." The chapter that covers Step Eleven in *Twelve Steps and Twelve Traditions* offers some good tidbits on meditation, as does *The Twelve Steps and Twelve Traditions of Overeaters Anonymous.* Another good AA book is *Came to Believe,* which contains the stories of how men and women, well, "came to believe." A great description of what is meant by a spiritual experience appears in "Spiritual Experience," in appendix 2 of the Big Book.

The Twelve Steps of recovery

You can't hang around OA for very long without hearing a lot about the Steps, as in "writing a Fourth Step" or "doing a Tenth Step." Many people say that the Steps are what separates OA from a diet club. Many OA Step Study meetings focus specifically on the Twelve Steps.

The Twelve Steps, like so much of the OA program, are taken directly from Alcoholics Anonymous, but a few changes were made to adapt them for compulsive overeaters. In OA's Step One we admit that we are powerless over *food,* and in OA's Step Twelve we carry the message to other *compulsive overeaters.*

Like everything else in the program, the Twelve Steps are suggestions; the program slogan "Take what you need and leave the rest" applies to the Steps as well. But as one friend of mine in the program said, "I noticed that everyone who had the kind of recovery I wanted was working the Steps, so I realized that I had better start working them too." Working the Steps doesn't guarantee happiness. But not working the Steps guarantees problems as you attempt to recover from overeating.

Here is my brief overview of the Steps. For more information, you should attend OA meetings that study the Steps, as well as read the program literature pertaining to the Steps. Good books about the Steps include *The Twelve Steps and Twelve Traditions of Overeaters Anonymous, Alcoholics Anonymous,* and the AA book *Twelve Steps and Twelve Traditions.* OA also puts out a nice workbook with questions designed to help you work each step.

❦ *Step work*

So how does one actually work the Steps? There are many different ways, but the Steps can't be done alone. They require a lot of work with other compulsive overeaters. It helps to have an OA sponsor who has worked all the Steps to guide you.

Before you can actually work the Steps, you have to know what they are. To begin, read the book *The Twelve Steps and Twelve Traditions of Overeaters Anonymous,* and then read at least the first 164 pages of the Big Book of AA. These readings will give you a good background on the Steps.

I usually recommend memorizing the Steps. It's not really that hard to do, especially since they are brief and are read so often at meetings. Committing them to memory makes it easier to "practice these principles in all our affairs."

Groups of overeaters sometimes get together outside of regular OA meetings to work through the Steps. Sometimes called A Way of Life, or AWOL, these groups differ from regular OA meetings in that they have specific requirements that put them outside of the Twelve Traditions. For example, the members agree to work the Steps together according to a given schedule. This includes writing the personal inventory by a certain date. The group may also agree to other rules regarding attendance and abstinence. I have been through two AWOL groups and have found them to be powerful.

Some of the Steps may seem difficult or impossible. Don't worry. Every single one of us has thought the same thing. If any one Step seems impossible, it just means that you aren't ready to take it. The Steps are meant to be worked in order, and you will find that after you do one Step the next one seems to follow almost naturally. Talk to other OA members to find out how they handled each Step. Don't let fear of the Steps keep you away from the OA program. As always, take what you need and leave the rest.

Step One: *We admitted we were powerless over food—that our lives had become unmanageable.*[*]

As the old saying goes, the longest journey starts with a single step. But until we take that first step, we can't go any further: we can't do anything

---

[*]Permission to use the Twelve Steps of Alcoholics Anonymous for adaptation granted to Overeaters Anonymous by AA World Services, Inc. The Twelve Steps of Overeaters Anonymous, as adapted, are reprinted with the permission of Overeaters Anonymous, Inc. (See editor's note on copyright page.)

about a problem we are unwilling to admit we have. For me, the First Step of OA means admitting that I have a problem with food. Since I used to be morbidly obese, this admission was relatively easy for me. I certainly would not have eaten the way I ate if I had had the power to control food all by myself, and I certainly wouldn't have weighed what I did.

The word *powerless* disturbs some people. Those who have struggled for years to gain self-esteem and win their rights may object to giving up what they have struggled for. But accepting the truth about ourselves doesn't mean giving up our rights or sense of self-worth—it just means we can start to recover from a serious eating disorder. One way of looking at powerlessness is to think of the effect that food has on us. We can't change the way our brain chemistry reacts to food, nor can we change the genes that we inherited. Another approach is to turn the word *powerless* into "less power." We have less power over food than other people.

Some fear that if they admit powerlessness they are doomed to nonstop bingeing for the rest of their lives. After all, is it not a contradiction to admit powerlessness over food and then try to stop overeating? No. Just because we have an eating disorder doesn't mean that we have to practice it. One OA member described it with a useful analogy: "I am powerless over the weather. I can't change whether it will rain or snow tomorrow. But I don't have to freeze to death."

Some of us also have qualms about the word *unmanageable.* When we manage something, we make decisions based on things in our control. For me, unmanageability means that practicing my addiction to food removed many of the choices and opportunities from my life that other people have, and thus made it unmanageable. I had virtually no choice about where I bought clothes because regular stores just didn't carry my size. I faced a great deal of employment discrimination because most potential employers seemed to judge me on my size rather than my ability. Moreover, my compelling cravings for excess food governed my life and thus made it unmanageable.

Step Two: *Came to believe that a Power greater than ourselves could restore us to sanity.*

Powerless doesn't mean hopeless. It just means that we can't do it by ourselves. People with kidney failure may be powerless over the fact that their kidneys won't take waste out of their blood, but with the help of dialysis, something outside of themselves, they can live reasonable lives. Likewise, just because we have an eating disorder doesn't mean that we are doomed to overeat for the rest of our lives.

Here is where what I call "generic god" starts to enter the picture. Don't panic. If a de facto heathen like I was could work this Step, you can too. OA doesn't demand that you believe in anybody else's concept of a

Higher Power. And keep in mind that OA isn't allied with any religious sect or denomination. I have met OA members who practice virtually every religion, including Catholicism, Protestantism, fundamentalism, Judaism, Buddhism, neopaganism, Islam, and atheism.

OA doesn't attempt to describe this "Power greater than ourselves." We aren't trained to be theologians, and we aren't competing with them. For most of us this is some type of a god, but it need not be. It only has to be greater than ourselves. Many OA members who have trouble believing in a god start out by using the group as their Higher Power, since the group collectively has a lot more experience and knowledge than any one of its members.

Also, your Higher Power need not be a "Him." The Steps refer to God as a he because that was the usual way of doing it fifty years ago, and OA has tried to make as few changes in the Steps as possible. You are free to use any conception of your own Higher Power that you want—whether it be he, she, it, or they.

For me, this Step really means that there is hope—even for me. I had never been thin in my life and I knew, mainly from my own sad experience, that most diets fail and that fat children grow up to be fat adults. But I got hope from attending OA meetings. There I found a group of people who were recovering from this hopeless disease! I met people who had lost more pounds than I had ever weighed, and who were maintaining that loss for years. I met bulimics who had been vomiting five times a day but recovered. I met people who were younger, older, richer, poorer, smarter, and dumber than I—all of whom were recovering. I even met a man who had once been a three-hundred-pound skid-row wino who ate out of garbage cans at fast-food restaurants. He had become a sober, productive, healthy-looking man. If people like that could do it, so could I.

Many people have problems with the use of the word *sanity,* thinking that it implies we are all crazy. Instead, I like to think of sanity as the ability to make sound choices about food. Bingeing right after I bought clothes in the fat store was certainly not an act of sanity. Continuing to eat as the stretch marks progressed across my body was not sane either.

Step Three: Made a decision to turn our will and our lives over to the care of God as we understood Him.

I interpret this Step as deciding to try OA, which is a spiritual program. I believe that anyone who stays past the Serenity Prayer at the first meeting has made a start on the first three Steps. They wouldn't be there if they did not have a problem, and they wouldn't stick around if they didn't think that working this spiritual program might help them. In other words, Steps One, Two, and Three.

Step Three is actually easier than it looks. All it says is that we made a decision. It doesn't say that we have joined a church or adopted any particular religion, simply that we have made a decision. It doesn't say that we have actually carried it out. For example, I could make a decision to go to Pittsburgh, but I don't have to plan when to go, where to stay, how to get there, or how to pay for the trip right now.

Many take Step Three by saying a beautiful prayer from the Big Book, which is sometimes used to close meetings. Just try not to gag with all of the "Thees" and "Thous."

> God, I offer myself to Thee—to build with me and to do with me as Thou wilt. Relieve me of the bondage of self, that I may better do Thy will. Take away my difficulties, that victory over them may bear witness to those I would help of Thy Power, Thy Love, and Thy Way of life. May I do Thy will always! [*]

My own experience with this Step was that I took it piecemeal. At first, I took it intellectually as something I knew I was going to have to do to work the Steps. It was a start. Then, one foggy Saturday afternoon I was at home alone in my apartment when I got the strongest feeling: *It's time.* I went to my room and said the Third Step Prayer and meant it for the first time. If you had told me that morning I was going to take Step Three that afternoon, I would have said you were crazy.

Of course, there is much more to Step Three than this. For further information, read the relevant OA and AA literature and attend Step meetings. Keep in mind that we aren't trying to convert you. If you have religious convictions, we urge you to practice them.

Step Four: Made a searching and fearless moral inventory of ourselves.

This Step is a critical part of the recovery process. Its purpose is to unearth the problems that made dealing with our eating disorder that much more difficult. In other words, what are our defects? One way of looking at our defects is to view them as behavior patterns that don't work anymore. Our survival demands that we face up to them and get rid of them. As it says in the Big Book, "A business which takes no regular inventory usually goes broke."[†] It must count up what it has and what it doesn't have, discover where the damaged merchandise is, and get rid of it.

I can't overstate the importance of this Step. Every single person I know in OA who has successfully maintained a large weight loss for a long time has taken this Step. Taking an inventory won't guarantee success, but not taking one will guarantee failure.

---

[*] *Alcoholics Anonymous,* 63.
[†] *Alcoholics Anonymous,* 64.

Some balk at it, saying, "But I have already gone through all of this stuff with my therapist!" If that's the case, and if you were really honest and thorough with your therapist, it should make this Step easy. It will then be a straightforward task to write your inventory and discuss it one more time. It's likely that you will learn even more useful things about yourself, since the process of self-exploration is never-ending. Even if you don't see a reason now for doing this Step, do it out of pragmatism—those with long-term recovery have done it and say that it's useful. Just do it and proceed with the rest of the Steps.

This Step doesn't say that our character defects caused our compulsive overeating. All it says is that we take a hard look at ourselves to find out where our problems are.

Uncovering problems. What kinds of problems are we likely to find? My own experience might be a guide. I have a lot of defects that made dealing with my eating disorder much more difficult than it had to be. This does not mean that I am a "bad" person; indeed, I am grateful to the program for teaching me that overeating isn't a moral issue. But my character defects were certainly an issue. For one thing, I was filled with denial, a form of dishonesty, about my disease. I denied that I had a problem with food. I foolishly thought that if other people didn't see me eat, it didn't count. I would go to great lengths to hide my binges, even though other people could tell by looking at me what I did with food. I would go to different stores on different days so that the clerks wouldn't see how much I was eating. If one of them happened to mention the food I was buying, I would deny that it was all for me. I always said I was having a party. I even denied the health consequences of my obesity by quoting studies that showed the insurance company height and weight charts were wrong and were about to be revised upward. They were revised upward by a few pounds, but I was still morbidly obese by any standard.

I was also filled with false pride. I thought I could do it by myself. After all, I was an expert on weight loss from my years of dieting. And I could count calories faster than an IBM 3090. Unfortunately, this knowledge didn't stop me from overeating.

I procrastinated a lot. My motto was "I'll go on my diet tomorrow . . . next Monday . . . next year." Moreover, I have a lot of run-of-the-mill defects like greed, lust, and envy.

My eating disorder, combined with my rationalizations—"I don't have a problem," "I can do it myself," and "I'll do it later"—led me to become severely overweight. The Fourth Step forced me to take a look inside myself and face these facts. My survival demands that I work on them.

By now you may be convinced of the absolute necessity of writing an inventory, but you may still wonder about the mechanics. The simplest advice is this: Get a pencil. Get some paper. Get honest. This means sit down and write some very personal things, such as a list of people you are angry with and why you are angry. Try writing a list of your fears, too, because they are usually instructive as to the nature of your defects. It's also useful to include a list of your deepest secrets, since it's often said that we are only as sick as our secrets. Then, use these lists to examine your character defects.

Some tips for taking this Step. There are many different guides to the Fourth Step. The questions in *The Twelve Steps and Twelve Traditions of Overeaters Anonymous* are thorough and provide a good start. Some formats are passed around among program members; other guides are available from outside publishers. You will find a lot of guidance in Chapter Five of the Big Book as well as in AA's *Twelve Steps and Twelve Traditions.* The abundance of different formats for taking the Fourth Step may confuse you; it did me. I stumbled around with many different ones before I settled on the one in the Big Book, but the format isn't as important as being thorough.

You may feel overwhelmed at the enormity of the task in Step Four. Relax and take the Step a little at a time. The inventory isn't meant to be a long autobiography—you don't have to account for every moment of your life. The purpose is to find out where the problems are, which you can do without writing hundreds of pages. On the other hand, there is nothing wrong with writing a long autobiography if it helps you identify problem areas.

Procrastination may rear its ugly head. If it does, don't forget to write it down! You may have the best intentions of writing but may never get around to it. It's too tempting to wait until your desk is clear and you find the perfect pen and the perfect paper. It helps to commit yourself to writing for five minutes each day, or to answer one question per day from a Fourth Step guide. Keep in mind that your inventory doesn't need to be of great literary merit, nor does it matter whether you write legibly or spell correctly.

Facing up to our problems may seem dreary, but it need not be. Remember that the purpose of the personal inventory is to find out where our problems are, not to lay blame. An inventory isn't an indictment of others or ourselves. It's not an exercise in self-flagellation. Most of us are already too good at beating ourselves up.

Don't ignore your good parts. Just as an accounting statement carries both assets and liabilities, so does a personal inventory. It's important to write down the good things about ourselves as well. Although we all have a lot of room for improvement, an inventory shouldn't focus on just our negative aspects.

There is no such thing as the perfect format or the perfect Fourth Step.

The important thing is to do your best. If you leave something out, as most of us do, you can always go back later to cover anything you omitted. Don't let perfectionism paralyze you in this Step.

I have done several inventories over the years and discovered important things about myself each time. The inventory process has been compared to peeling an onion—every time you peel off a layer, there is another layer beneath it. Some say that you need only do the Fourth Step once and that further inventories are really Tenth Steps, but I think that distinction is hairsplitting. It doesn't matter what number you call your inventory as long as you do it.

Don't worry about finding someone with whom to discuss your inventory. That comes in later Steps. If you decide now to give your inventory to a particular person, you may subconsciously begin to edit the material, which would be a mistake. The more fearless and thorough the inventory, the better.

A word of caution: If you do this Step well, you are bound to write things that you want to keep private. Be careful where you leave your writing. I once met a young man in the program who was working on a lengthy inventory that dealt with a lot of family resentments. Unfortunately, his mother found it and the misunderstanding led to a big family argument.

Once again, I can't overstate the importance of this Step. We can't even begin to deal with our problems until we know what they are, and this Step is an important tool for finding them out. Most of us were so anesthetized by excess food that we were unaware of many of our problems. It's not always pleasant to take out the garbage, especially if it hasn't been done for a long time and has begun to smell. But it's better to do it and be done with it than to pretend that it doesn't smell. Every single person who has the kind of recovery that I want has done this Step. I have seen many people who absolutely refused to do this Step, and invariably they went back to food.

Step Five: *Admitted to God, to ourselves, and to another human being the exact nature of our wrongs.*

Admitting that we have problems and that we are imperfect is an important part of our recovery. We continue our spiritual development with this Step by continuing to get honest. Most of us lied to ourselves about food: "I'll just have one bite. . . ." "I can stop whenever I want to. . . ." "I will start my diet tomorrow. . . ."

Step Five is another part of the process of recognizing what clergy and therapists have been telling us for years—talking about our problems is part of dealing with them. Typically, the Fifth Step is done by reading the inventory you wrote in the Fourth Step to someone. It can be your sponsor, therapist, religious counselor, friend, or any person you trust. Just make sure whoever you pick understands what you are trying to do and will respect your confidence. The recipient doesn't have to be in OA, although it's helpful if he or she is familiar with the program. If you are engaging the services of a professional, make sure that you schedule enough time for him or her to listen to and perhaps discuss your entire inventory. One hour may not be enough.

If the Fifth or any Step scares you, try not to worry about it. They scared all of us before we did them. If you are scared, it just means that you may not be ready to take the Step. There will come a time in your recovery when you realize that you must continue to progress in the Steps or you will probably return to overeating.

When I took the Fifth Step, I wondered why I needed to talk about my inventory with another human being. If I know about my problems, and I am sure God does, what difference does it make? There are two ways to answer this question: (1) Everyone who has what I want—sane, long-term maintenance—has done it. If I want what they have, I should do what they did. (2) Talking about my inventory with another person makes it seem more real. It's easy for me to delude myself. I may think I know what my problems are until I begin to get them on paper. Then the problems that I uncover take on much greater importance as I talk about them with another person.

Discussing our inventory with another person is cathartic, helping us get rid of things that have bothered us for a long time. Many of us have carried around a great deal of guilt about things we have done. These feelings fester inside us and take much of the joy out of life. Just talking about what happened can help us realize that we can't change the past, and that wallowing in guilt will do us no good. It allows us to put the past behind us and get on with life.

I have had the privilege of listening to several inventories. What has amazed me is that the secrets that seem to upset people most are generally minor. Talking about them with another person can help us to put these things in perspective. For example, you may feel guilty about a nasty thing you said when you were a child, even though the other person may have long forgotten the incident.

After it's read and discussed, the inventory is often burned or shredded. This is a symbol for getting rid of the resentments and character defects that it contains, as well as a practical way to make sure that it does not fall into the wrong hands. I met one person whose inventory was subpoenaed in a palimony lawsuit.

Step Six: *Were entirely ready to have God remove all these defects of character.*

Step Seven: *Humbly asked Him to remove our shortcomings.*

In Steps Four and Five we started to face up to our problems, but becoming aware of them doesn't make them go away. Just as we can't get rid of our addiction by ourselves, we also need help in getting rid of our character defects. Once you become aware of your defects in the earlier Steps, you eventually become sick and tired of them and want to change them to improve your life. In Step Seven you ask your Higher Power for help. These two Steps represent our willingness to let go of our defects and continue our spiritual development. Remember that we aren't talking about becoming goody-goodies; we are talking about getting rid of the flaws that made us so miserable.

Here is a lovely prayer from the Big Book for taking Step Seven that is sometimes used to end OA meetings:

> My Creator, I am now willing that you should have all of me, good and bad. I pray that you now remove from me every single defect of character which stands in the way of my usefulness to you and my fellows. Grant me strength, as I go out from here, to do your bidding. Amen.[*]

In my experience, these two Steps are the most painful. When I first heard the Twelve Steps, I realized that talking about my problems with another human being and making amends were going to be difficult, but asking to have your problems removed didn't sound too bad. Indeed, reading the Big Book's discussions makes it sound simple—just take an hour after you give away your inventory, make sure that you left nothing out, and then ask God to take your defects away.[†]

But the kickers in Step Six are the words *entirely* and *all.* Most of us are willing to have our most inconvenient problems removed. But we aren't willing to have God remove *all* our defects of character, just the most painful ones. We may want to hang on to some of our defects because we fear what we would be like without them. I have heard that we'll know we are ready to take Steps Six and Seven when we feel like we're in a dirty diaper and beg for it to be changed.

Note that nowhere in the Steps does it say that we got rid of our character defects or that all our character defects went away. Far from it. All we did was ask that these shortcomings be removed. It's up to our Higher Power to decide whether and/or when to do so.

---

[*] *Alcoholics Anonymous,* 76.
[†] *Alcoholics Anonymous,* 75.

Step Eight: *Made a list of all persons we had harmed and became willing to make amends to them all.*

Step Nine: *Made direct amends to such people wherever possible, except when to do so would injure them or others.*

At first, it may seem hard to see how these two Steps apply to overeaters. It's clear that many alcoholics have done a lot of damage that needs to be repaired. Barroom fights, smashed cars, and ruined careers are all stereotypical consequences of alcoholism. As overeaters, we generally don't have these same things hanging over our heads. If we isolated ourselves in our disease, we may have less dramatic damage to amend. Yet, our families have often borne the brunt of our disease. And we caused a lot of pain to those who care about us by not being emotionally present for them because we were stoned on food. Since many of our family members are also addicts of various types, we often aided and abetted their self-destruction too. We may also carry the guilt of having taught our children to behave destructively with food.

One of the great things about making amends is that it helps us get rid of old guilt. After making amends, we feel cleaner about ourselves and thus have one less painful emotion that may tempt us to overeat.

In addition, making amends helps to patch up our relationships with others. When we treat other people in an honest and straightforward manner, they are much more likely to treat us in the same way. Making amends also sends a strong signal to others that we have changed. Our friends and family have watched our many futile attempts to control food in the past and are justifiably skeptical when we join OA. But making amends lets them know that this time we are serious about changing. When they see this, they will be much more supportive. This tends to calm the emotional storms that sometimes surround our life and influence us to seek refuge in overeating.

Making amends isn't only a signal to others that you have changed, but also a signal to yourself. By making sometimes difficult amends for the past, you acknowledge to yourself that your recovery is worth working for. You are much more likely to hold on to something when you have worked hard to get it.

To make amends we usually speak to the person face-to-face, sincerely apologize for what we have done, and then do what we can to fix the harm. Some of the people on your amends list may be not be available for a face-to-face chat. If so, write them a letter. If the person has died or can't be found, write a letter to him or her anyway. The real point isn't to talk, but to actually become willing to change our behavior so that we don't do the same things anymore.

People will react in many different ways to your amends. Some are amazed that anyone would try to clear up something that happened so long ago. Some gladly accept your amends; others who are still angry over what you did to them may be hostile. Some may not feel they have been wronged and may be quite confused as to why you are apologizing.

Remember two key points: (1) Make sure that you do no further harm in the process, especially if third parties are involved. For example, making amends by apologizing to the unknowing partner of the person with whom you had an affair may cause great harm. (2) Amends are needed only when you have actually harmed people, not merely resented them. It's a tremendous abuse of the program to walk up to a person and say "I need to make amends to you because I resented you for being such a jerk yesterday." It's a good idea to check with your sponsor before making any amends to make sure that amends are needed.

There may be some people to whom you owe amends who have harmed you as well. You may be unwilling to do anything for someone you feel owes you an apology. But remember that amends are for repairing the harm that *you* have done. You will feel better knowing that you have cleaned up your part of the situation.

Don't forget to include yourself on the amends list. We overeaters have done ourselves a great deal of harm by abusing our bodies with excess food. We have treated ourselves worse than we would have treated our worst enemies. But how do we make amends to ourselves for all the years of self-abuse? *By not doing it anymore.* Eating just the right amount of healthy food, neither too much nor too little, is really the best way of making amends to ourselves.

You may be confused about whether you have completed your amends. A good rule of thumb is that you are finished if you can think of no one who meets the following test: If a certain person were walking down the street, would you be tempted to go out of your way to avoid him or her because of what you had done?

Step Ten: *Continued to take personal inventory and when we were wrong, promptly admitted it.*

This Step is just plain old common sense. We continue to be aware of what is really going on in our lives and promptly and honestly clean up our mistakes. Step Ten reasserts the need for rigorous honesty by taking inventory and admitting mistakes. The ongoing effort to uncover and deal with our problems is important for us because it's very easy to slip into complacency and deadly denial of our problems. Admitting mistakes quickly is often the easiest way to deal with them. We don't have to pretend to be omnipotent, and we can de-escalate potentially serious situations by demonstrating that we are dealing in good faith. Besides, the humility it takes to admit a mistake is a reminder that we don't run the universe.

There are many ways to work Step Ten. Some people write a mini-inventory each day, but I am too lazy for that. Nightly I do a spot-check inventory to find out where I am physically, emotionally, and spiritually. (See p. 86.) But I must admit that on some days I drift off to sleep before I finish the inventory.

Spot-check inventory. Another good spot-check is to run down the tools of the program to see what is missing. Try this form.

- *Abstinence.* On a scale of one to one hundred—with one meaning violent bingeing and one hundred meaning you couldn't possibly think of any improvements in your food—how would you rate your food today?
- *Meetings.* How many OA meetings have you attended in the last month? In the last week?
- *Service.* Do you have a service job at an OA meeting?
- *Sponsorship.* Do you have a sponsor? How many times in the past week have you talked to your sponsor? Are you sponsoring anyone? If so, how often have you spoken with him or her in the past week?
- *Telephone calls.* How many OA phone calls have you made today? In the last seven days?
- *Literature.* When was the last time you read any of the OA or AA literature? How many pages have you read in the last week? In the last month? Do you read OA's *Lifeline* magazine?
- *Writing.* How much writing have you done in the last week?
- *Anonymity.* Are you putting principles before personalities, or are you getting hung up on who said what to whom?
- *Prayer and meditation.* How is your conscious contact with your Higher Power? Did you pray today? Did you meditate today?
- *Resentments.* Are you angry or resentful at anyone? Why?
- *Major events.* What happened today, and how do you feel about it? Are any of your character defects active?
- *Step work.* How is your practice of the Twelve Steps coming along?

Step Eleven: *Sought through prayer and meditation to improve our conscious contact with God* as we understood Him, *praying only for knowledge of His will for us and the power to carry that out.*

Continuing to work on our spiritual development is an important part of recovering from compulsive overeating. I don't have to know why prayer and meditation work. All I know is that I feel better when I pray and meditate. When I don't, I feel less serene and more agitated.

The only thing I can say about prayer and meditation is, Try it, you'll like it. The only risk is that it might work. It doesn't matter if you don't believe in a Higher Power. Act as if and see if it doesn't help. As one OA member put it, "There may not be anything up there, but if that's the case Nothing is running my life better than I could."

There are many different ways to pray. You can use prayers that others have written, or you can use your own. OA isn't a religious program and thus provides very little guidance on how to pray or to whom. For more guidance here, I suggest that you follow the teachings of your choice.

There are a lot of useful prayers around. I have found the Serenity Prayer, which is used to begin most OA meetings, is good for getting past treacherous foods in the grocery store.[*]

Another favorite is the prayer attributed to St. Francis:

> Lord, make me a channel of thy peace—that where there is hatred, I may bring love—that where there is wrong, I may bring the spirit of forgiveness—that where there is discord, I may bring harmony—that where there is error, I may bring truth—that where there is doubt, I may bring faith—that where there is despair I may bring hope—that where there are shadows I may bring light—that where there is sadness I may bring joy. Lord, grant that I may seek rather to comfort than to be comforted—to understand, than to be understood—to love, than to be loved. For it is by self-forgetting that one finds. It is by forgiving that one is forgiven. It is by dying that one awakens to Eternal Life. Amen.[†]

In addition to prayer, Step Eleven talks about meditation. As a matter of fact, it says "prayer *and* meditation" (italics mine), not "prayer *or* mediation." This means that we need to do both.

There are many ways to meditate, and I don't pretend to be an expert on the subject. Some of the best advice I have been given is simple: Sit still. Be quiet. Don't ask. Don't answer. For more suggestions, follow the time-tested traditions of the religion of your choice. Another source that helped me is the book *How to Meditate* by Lawrence LeShan.

I usually meditate immediately after my morning prayers. I sit still, close my eyes, and try to keep my mind blank. It's difficult to keep my mind blank when thoughts of the day come to intrude. I often recite the Twelve Steps to myself so I don't forget them. At other times, I do a breath-counting exercise where I count my breaths in cycles from one to four. I might also imagine myself in a place of great natural beauty and tranquil-

---

[*]The Serenity Prayer is attributed to Reinhold Niebuhr. The form said at meetings is a truncated form of a longer prayer.
[†] *Twelve Steps and Twelve Traditions* (New York, N.Y.: Alcoholics Anonymous World Services, Inc., 1981), 99.

ity, such as a forest or a beach, and try to absorb some of that beauty and tranquility.

I try to meditate for at least five minutes each day. It may not sound like much, but it's something that I can stick with, and that's important—your prayer and meditation must be something you can work into your everyday life. Whenever I tried to allocate thirty minutes a day to meditating, it ended up like all of my previous exercise programs: I would start off with great enthusiasm for a few days, but I would soon lose my commitment and forget about it. By starting small, I ensure that I get at least something done.

Step Twelve: *Having had a spiritual awakening as the result of these steps, we tried to carry this message to compulsive overeaters and to practice these principles in all our affairs.*

When I first heard this Step I nearly bolted for the door. So that was it! They were going to turn me into a Moonie. I envisioned myself standing at the airport, passing out literature like my high school friend who joined the Hare Krishna. Or maybe I would have some kind of vision and hear voices. Fortunately, OA doesn't work like that. This Step involves putting our new way of living into action and helping our fellow compulsive overeaters.

Step Twelve is the only Step that gets its own chapter, "Working with Others," in the Big Book. And the chapter on Step Twelve in *Twelve Steps and Twelve Traditions* is the longest in the book. In OA, we are carrying the message to other compulsive overeaters. In order to recover from overeating, we have to work with other overeaters.

First of all, we have to have had a spiritual awakening. What do we mean by that? How do we know if we have had one? Spiritual experiences mean different things to different people. Sometimes they are sudden realizations; other times they are gradual changes. They allow us to do and feel things that we were unable to before, to tap into that Power greater than ourselves that we had not tapped into before.

Some consider a spiritual awakening a fundamental change in attitude toward life, as when a self-centered addict begins to reach out to others. Indeed, some alcoholics say that AA stands for "attitude adjustment."

My spiritual awakening has been a gradual realization that I don't run the universe. I don't pretend to understand the inner workings of God. I don't have to. I know that there is a Power greater than I, even if I don't understand it. My attitude toward life has changed significantly. I am no longer as impatient or self-centered as I used to be. My awakening has been of the "educational variety" described in the Big Book.[*]

---

[*] *Alcoholics Anonymous*, 569-70.

How do we have one of these experiences? Actually, it's not mysterious. The Steps are a proven method for having a spiritual awakening. By admitting the truth to ourselves about our food addiction, by becoming willing to follow a spiritual path, by cleaning up the wreckage from our past, and by seeking spiritual growth through prayer and meditation, we will have a spiritual awakening. Note that Step Twelve says "as *the* result of these Steps" not "as *a* result of these Steps."

The spirituality of OA isn't about mystical experiences on a mountaintop. It's about putting my faith into action by trying to help other compulsive overeaters. By passing on what has been given to me, I remind myself of where I came from and get another reprieve from complacency—the deadly enemy of every recovering compulsive overeater. It's very easy for me to fool myself that I am now cured, that I can now eat like a "normal" person. I can also fool myself into thinking that my compulsive overeating wasn't so bad. Then, when I work with newcomers and see their pain, I remember how it was for me and I become grateful for what I have.

When we talk about working with others in OA, we mean other people who want to recover from overeating. Our job isn't to convince people to lose weight or to drag jolly fat people out of bakeries, but to help ourselves by helping those who want that help.

We carry the OA message in many ways. We do it by going to meetings where we see what works and doesn't work for other overeaters. We do it when we tell other overeaters what worked for us and remind ourselves of what we need to do. And we do it through sponsorship, both having a sponsor and being one.

Finally, we seek to practice these principles in all of our affairs. But just what are these principles? The book *The Twelve Steps and Twelve Traditions of Overeaters Anonymous* has a nice summary of the principles that are involved with each of the Twelve Steps:

❦ *The principles in the Twelve Steps*

1. Honesty	5. Integrity	9. Love
2. Hope	6. Willingness	10. Perseverance
3. Faith	7. Humility	11. Spiritual awareness
4. Courage	8. Self-Discipline	12. Service[*]

There is more to the Twelve Steps than I have been able to comprehend in ten years or pass on in these few pages. The Steps are really a commonsense way of living for a recovering addict like me. They teach me to deal honestly with myself and others. Most importantly, they teach me how to live daily without excess food.

---

[*] *The Twelve Steps and Twelve Traditions of Overeaters Anonymous,* 103-6.

Twelve Traditions

The pioneers of AA developed the Twelve Traditions through many years of trial and error as they figured out how to keep groups of addicts from self-destructing. Here is an overview of how the Traditions direct the operations of OA, organized according to some of the themes that guide the Traditions. (For a more complete picture, refer to *The Twelve Steps and Twelve Traditions of Overeaters Anonymous* and to the AA book *Twelve Steps and Twelve Traditions*.)

Two major themes in the traditions are anonymity and simplicity. As mentioned in Tradition Twelve, anonymity "is the spiritual foundation of all these traditions." This reinforces the basic OA principle that we get better by helping other overeaters like ourselves without thinking about personal rewards. Thus, we stay anonymous in public and do our best to put principles before personalities within the fellowship, as hard as that can sometimes be. This principle of humble service is reflected in the fact that OA has no governors who can give orders or expel members, and that there are no ranks (like the Salvation Army) or degrees (like the Masons).

The slogan "Keep it simple" represents another major theme. By focusing on only one thing and avoiding outside entanglements and controversies, OA can thrive with the least possible organizational complexity.

In the spirit of "First things first," Tradition One urges unity within the program, since bitter debate and controversy divert members' energies away from recovering. Not only do the Traditions warn against internal dissension, but Tradition Ten also frowns upon getting involved in outside controversies. Taking sides in public controversy inevitably alienates someone and may needlessly offend overeaters who need the program.

According to Tradition Three, anybody who wants to stop eating compulsively can be an OA member, so OA members don't have to waste precious time arguing about who belongs and who doesn't. No one can be kicked out for not having been heavy enough, not following a particular diet, or not paying dues (even if we had weight requirements, food plans, or dues, which we don't). However, even though almost anyone can join, that does not mean that OA tries to be all things to all people. According to Tradition Five, OA focuses its energy on helping the still-suffering compulsive overeater. By specializing in one thing, OA can do it well with a minimum of administrative overhead.

OA preserves its independence by refusing to (a) affiliate or endorse any outside enterprise, no matter how good (Tradition Six), and (b) accept any outside contributions (Tradition Seven). After all, outside money always comes with strings attached. Thus, OA does not sell a line of diet food, endorse a particular hospital treatment program, or beg for outside grants. This helps OA to maintain credibility, since it means that we are never going to be shills for some food company selling diet junk food. Furthermore, it avoids the institutional hassles that would come from trying to administer some type of affiliation.

Four of the Traditions (Two, Four, Eight, and Nine) deal with how the program is structured and who has what power. Tradition Two affirms that God is the ultimate authority, expressed through the group conscience. OA does not have a president who sets policy for the group and orders people around. This intentional lack of power in leaders is emphasized in Tradition Nine: there are no ranks, no hierarchy, no chain of command. Tradition Eight stipulates that OA not charge for its services or compete with any professionals.

Groups can do anything they want under Tradition Four, as long as they follow the Twelve Steps and Twelve Traditions of Overeaters Anonymous and are not doing things that hurt other groups or the overall fellowship. This is one reason why individual OA meetings vary so. Local autonomy also allows OA to evolve through trial and error to find the most effective means of helping overeaters in a survival-of-the-fittest manner. Each group is free to innovate in the ways that it thinks best. When the innovations succeed, other groups will copy them and they will spread throughout the fellowship. Innovations that do not succeed will eventually be abandoned.

Group decisions are usually made by holding regular business (or "group conscience") meetings, typically once a month after the regular meeting. All group members are invited to participate in the decision making. Local groups send delegates to an "intergroup" to make business decisions for a local area, such as printing a meeting list or answering the phone. There are also regional and world business meetings composed of delegates from the local areas. The annual World Service Business Conference acts as the group conscience for OA as a whole and handles items that concern the whole fellowship, such as approving official OA literature.

Traditions Eleven and Twelve deal with anonymity. There are two Traditions for dealing with anonymity, one for public relations and one for within the fellowship. Within the fellowship, anonymity means that we attempt to place principles before personalities, although from time to time that can be quite a challenge, given some of the personalities. In practice, OA members are urged not to use their last names in the media or allow their full faces to be used in pictures or on TV. However, there is absolutely nothing wrong with using last names within the fellowship. Likewise, it is not a "breach" of anonymity to tell a friend or co-worker that you are in Overeaters Anonymous. OA is an anonymous program, not a secret society.

Anonymity in the media shows the world how seriously we guard each person's privacy. This also protects a member from the glare of publicity; being in the news because of a large weight loss may overinflate our egos and make us think that we know all the answers, when we really don't. Since anyone can join OA, anonymity also guards the program from self-appointed spokespersons using OA to promote their own ideas on nutrition or other matters. Similarly, anonymity shields the fellowship from members who may wish to involve the OA name with other enterprises which may or may not be consistent with the principles of OA and which association may tarnish the image of OA in the public mind.

III
Continuing to Grow

Whether I have been abstinent twelve hours or twelve years,
I never have it made.
Today's recovery is all I have.
—*For Today*

Maintenance:
What happens after the weight loss?

Maintaining goal weight presents a new set of problems. Indeed, this is where many of us faltered after previous weight-loss attempts. We followed a strange diet or a compulsive exercise scheme until we lost the weight. But when we got to that magic number on the scale, we thought we were cured, so we celebrated by returning to overeating and regained our weight.

In Overeaters Anonymous, we learn to handle maintenance. We learn how to deal with the problems of adjusting to a new body size without returning to compulsive overeating.

❦ Not everything gets better
Many of us thought that all our problems would be solved by losing weight. I suspect that my own case is rather typical. I had never been thin before, so I had great illusions about what it was like to be thin. I thought that when I got thin I would be so handsome I'd have to fight off the women with a stick. I was going to be six feet tall and a millionaire. I also thought that I'd be able to eat whatever I wanted to whenever I wanted to.

Unfortunately, there is neither a pot of gold nor a pot of food at the end of the weight-loss rainbow. When I got thin, I realized that I was never going to be six feet tall and that I was still doomed to work for a living. I was as shy and socially awkward as I had always been. To make matters worse, since I had blamed all of my problems on my weight, all of my excuses disappeared. Now I was faced with the task of living my life.

Losing the weight had been a goal of mine ever since I was ten years old. Now that I had finally done it, what was I supposed to do next? How could I keep from gaining it back? What changes should I make in my food plan?

On the day that I hit goal, there was no earthquake. No chorus of angels appeared in the heavens singing "Alleluia." The passengers on the streetcar in San Francisco looked as sleepy as they always did at 7:00 A.M., and the security guards at work were as surly as they always were. My then girlfriend wasn't even talking to me.

It takes a long time to adjust to all the changes that take place after losing a lot of weight. Even though I have been maintaining for over a decade, I am still going through adjustments. Like many people, I went through all sorts of craziness after I hit goal. Fortunately, OA has numerous people who have been through it and can lend a sympathetic ear, and sometimes even some helpful advice.

The first area of craziness was about food. For what seemed like all my life, I had been trying to lose weight, but now it was time to stop. After decades of unsuccessful dieting, I had finally found a program that was working for me, and I had been adhering faithfully to my food plan. The thought of making any changes in it frightened me. It had worked so well, the weight had come off, and working the OA program had taken away the craving for excess food. There were many foods that I had not eaten while losing weight because I didn't know if they would set off a craving for more food. Should I try them in my food plan? The thought frightened me. What if I ate something that set off a craving? Would I be able to survive it, or would I relapse and never recover? On the other hand, I had visions of being able to eat lots of food after I hit goal. Since I didn't have to lose weight anymore, why should I deprive myself?

❦ Food plan changes

I got advice from other OA members to make changes in my food plan slowly and to work them out carefully with my sponsor. I was too impatient to work things out slowly, but I was fortunate to have an enlightened sponsor who gave me the room to make the mistakes I needed to make.

Being analytical, I calculated from my rate of weight loss precisely how many calories I could add to my food plan. I then proceeded to plan my first day on the new food plan. I added all the extra calories to dinner and told my sponsor exactly what I had planned. Fortunately, he had enough wisdom to let me try this. I prepared this huge amount of food and thought to myself that I would never be able to finish it. I told myself that I would eat until I felt full. About halfway through the meal, I realized that I was no longer hungry, but I kept saying to myself, *I'll just have one more bite.* Before I knew it, I ate the entire plate of food, but I still didn't feel full. Then it hit me—that old, sickening, stuffed feeling. I was afraid. Had I just binged? Was I still abstinent? Would I relapse and gain my weight back? I talked about it with my sponsor and he calmed me down. He reassured me that I didn't have to relapse and gain back the weight if I continued to work the program.

That was one of the mistakes I made when I hit maintenance, but it was one I had to make. I had to find out many of these things for myself. I tried all kinds of crazy food concoctions in hopes of creating the perfect meal. Have you ever tried to make cookies out of soy flour and Sweet'n Low? Fortunately, I worked closely with my sponsor, who was very patient with me and allowed me to see for myself that the answer was not in the food.

It's often said that when we hit goal weight, we need a little more food and a lot more program. How true! When we hit our goal weight before OA, the temporary nature of dieting always destroyed us. How do we keep from repeating our old mistake of winning the war but losing the peace?

The answer lies in the OA program. Because the weight was merely a symptom of our overeating, removing the symptom won't cure the problem. Whatever was wrong with my appestat is still wrong. What I need is a way of living without excess food.

That way of life takes a long time to develop. It's a long, slow journey that sometimes seems impossible. But it is possible, and anyone who has the willingness to start can do it. It requires a thorough overhaul of our personality, a change which is the result of working the Twelve Steps of the OA program.

❦ Questions about what to eat

The question of what to eat when you have hit goal weight is a big one. It's like the question of what to eat while losing the weight. The answer isn't very different, either. You still have to decide what to eat, how much to eat, and when to eat.

After I hit goal weight, I went through about a year and a half of what I call experimental eating. I wasn't too sure about what to eat and what not to eat, so within the framework of three meals a day and no sugar, I experimented with many different foods and styles of eating. I discovered the hard way that I couldn't eat certain foods, such as bread, rice, or potatoes. It seemed that whenever I added them to my food plan, I felt more cravings than I did at other times. I don't know why. Perhaps it's a physical reaction in my body or a product of the way I was raised. The reason does not matter to me today. Common sense tells me that if something makes me feel crazy when I eat it, I am better off not eating it.

I also tried "moderate mealing," or eating until I was "full" three times a day, instead of measuring my food. For some people, especially those who were never morbidly obese, it sometimes seems to work. For me, it was a great way to gain weight quickly. I returned to planning my meals in advance and measuring my food most of the time.

By the time I got rid of the foods that seemed to cause problems and settled into a style of eating I could stick with, I found that my food plan bore a slight resemblance to that ancient OA food plan that was once written on a gray sheet of paper. The pioneers of OA who created that plan were on to something. And I suspect there is a good reason why so many people in the program swear by it.

I have had my food plan computer-analyzed many times to make sure that I am getting all the vitamins and minerals I need, as well as the appropriate balance of protein, carbohydrates, and fat. I have also discussed my food plan with several doctors and nutritionists over the years, and they have assured me that I am indeed eating in a healthy way. When one of my doctors looked at my low cholesterol count and excellent state of health, he told me, "I wish I could get all of my patients to eat like you do."

❧ Healing emotional damage

When we reach maintenance, we need to deal with more than just the physical side of our disease. We lived as fat people for such a long time that many of us didn't know what it was like to be thin. Indeed, sometimes our body image may be so distorted that we don't realize we are thin. When I got close to my goal weight, people would tell me that I was thin, but I didn't believe them. I thought they were flattering me to get something out of me because people had been doing that to me for years when I was a fat person.

The emotional issues that come up when we hit goal weight are similar to the those that come up after we stop overeating. We still need to deal with our feelings without the delusion that food will fix our problems. We still need to deal with the pain, sorrow, and joy that life bestows on us. And we still need to continue to work on our spirituality, for that's what we have found to be the best way for dealing with our fears, our resentments, and our character defects.

A few emotional issues become more acute when you reach your goal weight. You may have a lost feeling of "Now what do I do with myself?" For me, losing the weight had been one of my major goals in life. Every time I wrote in my diary what I wanted to do over the next five years, losing weight was at the top of the list. After I lost the weight, I had to do some hard thinking about where my life was headed and what I wanted to do with it.

At this point, the reality of the eating disorder finally hits home. Admitting to ourselves that this is a lifelong problem makes us willing to continue working the Steps, which we need for lifelong recovery from compulsive overeating.

Relationship concerns come up in a big way when we reach our goal weight. Since many of us spent more time with food than people, there may be a sense of having lost time in the dating game, and a desire to make up for it quickly. Some of us expected the perfect mate to show up on the day we hit our goal weight; most of us were disappointed. We discovered that although we were now more attractive, we still had to go through the uncertainties, pains, and pleasures that most people go through in dating. Fearful that our thin size wouldn't last long, it was tempting to grab the first person to walk by, no matter how wrong the fit.

Another surprise is that total strangers treat us like normal people. Many of us thought, *This person doesn't know I am really a fat person.* Some of us developed instant resentments to some of our new acquaintances, thinking, *This person wouldn't have wanted to be around me when I was fat.*

It generally takes about a year for the emotional craziness to settle down. As we continue to go to meetings, talk with other overeaters, and work on our spiritual development through the Twelve Steps, much of the craziness fades and is replaced with serenity and contentment. The Promises[*] of the program do come true: "We are going to know a new freedom and a new happiness. . . . We will comprehend the word serenity and we will know peace."

❧ Healing physical damage

Those of us who have lost enormous amounts of weight can attest to the resulting health benefits. My blood pressure has declined and my cholesterol level is very low. My back gives me much less trouble than it used to, and I can climb several flights of stairs without having to stop to catch my breath. My complexion is better and I no longer get cysts and rashes. But a lot of damage remains.

For those of us who had been fat all our lives, we had exaggerated notions about what would happen after we lost the weight. For one thing, we thought that we would have a cosmetically perfect body that looked like a model's. Wrong. There remains damage to our bodies that doesn't go away.

For example, stretch marks. Normally, when your body changes size, your skin is elastic enough to stretch. But those of us with stretch marks

---

[*]*Alcoholics Anonymous*, 83-84.

gained so much weight that our skin couldn't stretch or grow fast enough to hold it. So the skin started forming bright red scar tissue, which typically started in the abdomen and the arms and then spread everywhere.

I first started getting stretch marks when I was fourteen. I didn't know what they were. I thought they might be cancer or some strange disease, so I went to a dermatologist. He explained what they were and then threw in, "Pregnant women get them all the time." That was just the thing a teenage male needed to hear.

When the weight comes off, the stretch marks don't just disappear. Instead, like other scars, they slowly fade from bright red or purple into tiny white slashes. But they don't go away. Even after years of maintaining a normal size, my scars are still visible.

The same is true for the loose skin that remains after a large weight loss. Our skin doesn't automatically shrink back to a normal size. Some of it may firm up, but most of it doesn't, even after years of exercise. The "goo" remains.

Fertility problems also seem common among people in the program, although I don't know if they are more frequent in OA than elsewhere. Years of abusing our bodies with junk food binges and starvation diets have taken their toll. Many women, particularly those who have been anorexic, have had menstrual difficulties. These often clear up as women abstain from over- and undereating, but sometimes they don't. Some women who attempt to lose too much weight stop menstruating, but then start again when their weight returns to normal. When this happens, a woman should seek prompt medical advice.

Some of us also get sensitive to cold after we lose weight. We were so used to carrying around extra insulation on our bodies that when it's gone we get cold easily. I suspect that our bodies are fighting the loss of all those calories by turning down our internal thermostats. Also, we are no longer attempting to dump thousands of extra calories by burning them off as heat, although we were never able to burn them all off.

Even years after the extra weight is gone, some damage remains. It's possible to have reconstructive surgery to repair some of the external body damage; the loose skin, for example, can be removed and tightened up. Although I haven't had such surgery, there are those in OA who have, and you can talk to them and learn from their experience.

Traps to avoid

On your road to recovery, you can fall into many traps. Your eating disorder may lie dormant for a long time, just waiting to strike when you are vulnerable. I have observed that many OA members—and sometimes entire OA groups—fall into these traps. A few are presented here as a warning.

❧ *The diet club trap*

Newcomers often make the mistake of treating OA like a diet club whose sole purpose is to help them lose weight. They tend to ignore everything but losing weight and don't realize that the program is really about living with an eating disorder without practicing the disease. Often, their physical recovery seems to stand in the way of their ability to absorb the rest of the program. If they are losing weight, they think they know how the program works and ignore the rest of it: "How dare you tell me that I am not doing it the right way—I've lost thirty pounds in the last six months!"

Unfortunately, those who try to diet without making any other changes usually return to overeating, often gaining all their weight back and then some. This may be what it takes to make them realize that there is more to OA than following a food plan.

We need to remember that our disease affects us emotionally and spiritually, as well as physically, and that we have to recover on all three levels. A common pitfall is to focus on one area, exclude the others, and thus lose balance. An old OA riddle goes: Which part of recovery is more important—the physical, the emotional, or the spiritual? Answer: The part that's missing. Another way to remember to keep balanced in the program is to view recovery as a three-legged stool that supports our life. One leg is physical, one emotional, and one spiritual. If any leg is missing, the stool tips over.

❧ *The fat serenity trap*

This trap is the opposite of the diet club trap. Members become so satisfied with their emotional and spiritual progress that they ignore the physical side and remain dangerously overweight. Health complications—hypertension, diabetes, heart disease, back and joint troubles—can make this trap lethal.

I have seen many people who are overwhelmed by the love and acceptance they find in the fellowship. For most of us, it's the first time that we felt we fit in anywhere. We were relieved to learn that we weren't stupid, weak-willed gluttons and that our overeating wasn't a moral issue. Nevertheless, this emotional progress will be stunted if the physical progress is stunted. Many overeaters pause during their recovery until they once more get "sick and tired of being sick and tired" and feel enough pain to work the entire program.

❧ *The complacency trap*

Complacency can hit anyone who thinks that he or she has it made. Because our disease never goes away, we need to be aware of it constantly and continue to take the steps to maintain our recovery. It's often tempting to think when we reach a normal weight and maintain it for a long time that we are "normal." The sad reality is that we can still dig our graves with our forks and we had better not forget it.

As George Santayana said, "Those who cannot remember the past are condemned to repeat it." Unfortunately, that's what happens to someone who gets too complacent and lets his or her program slip. The feeling of "It can't happen to me" is dangerous because it will tempt you to slack off on your recovery and make relapse more likely. Relapses don't strike out of the blue. Usually, they approach slowly and with warnings that are too often ignored.

❦ *The know-it-all trap*

It's easy for some of us to think that we know all the answers and that we don't have to listen to the experience of others. As graduates and dropouts of countless diet programs, we have spent many years attempting to deal with our eating disorder. We know this food is good and that one is bad. We know why we overate, or at least on whom we can blame our overeating. Our pride says that we can control our eating disorder without doing those things that the real sickos have to do—like go to meetings or read all that stuff that was written by alcoholics. We don't need any of that prayer stuff, either.

Since we already know the answers, we ignore the experience of those who have gone before us. But our old ways of thinking and acting don't work when it comes to dealing with food. Trust me, it's a lot easier to recover if we keep an open mind and do what we see working for others like us.

Sometimes it seems as if smart people have a harder time of it in OA. Perhaps we are used to figuring everything out for ourselves, figuring out all the angles for beating the system. But if we bring that same attitude to bear in our recovery, it gets us nowhere. Remember that our best efforts at fixing ourselves had failed. Our unaided intelligence and willpower, strong as they were, couldn't conquer our eating disorder. If we think that we don't have to do all the things that other people do to recover—like attending lots of OA meetings and working the Steps—then the results are usually dismal.

I remember at one time I was sponsoring both a doctor and a cab driver. The doc was having a hard time getting better because he kept insisting on doing things his way and not going to OA meetings. The cab driver had a much easier time because he followed the suggested program of OA.

Many alcoholics who are compulsive overeaters fall into this trap. After years of sobriety in AA, they come into OA to deal with their eating disorder, thinking overcoming food will be easy compared to booze. After all, what is a cookie compared with demon rum? And haven't they been living the Twelve Steps for so many years?

One mistake that "double winners" make is that they regard their AA program as a complete substitute for the OA program. They go to a few OA meetings and then attempt to diet. They don't realize that food addiction is an additional disorder that must be taken seriously. They think they know everything there is to know about Twelve Step programs because of their long AA sobriety, so why bother going to OA? Perhaps they misunderstand the foundation of their recovery.

Chapter Seven of the Big Book states it bluntly (I've made the usual substitutions): "Practical experience shows that nothing will so much insure immunity from [overeating] as intensive work with other [overeaters]. It works when other activities fail."[*] This means working with others who have our disease. Not everyone in AA has an eating disorder, and those who don't are as baffled by eating disorders as nonalcoholics are baffled by alcoholism. Simply put, you have to work with other compulsive overeaters to recover from compulsive overeating.

Many alcoholics who are also overeaters report that their craving for alcohol diminished rapidly when they started abstaining from overeating. They say they felt no desire for alcohol when their food was in order. Some alcoholics seem to be especially sensitive to sweets. Eating sugary junk food causes their blood sugar level to rise dramatically, and then crash as the body overcompensates. This low-blood-sugar level causes tiredness and irritability, and for many alcoholics, the desire to drink. A good food plan can help to alleviate the physical craving for both food and alcohol.

❦ The star syndrome

This syndrome is an easy one to fall into. A compulsive overeater joins OA and immediately starts shedding pounds. The physical recovery may be so rapid and spectacular that it outruns the emotional and spiritual recovery. The newcomer is bombarded with compliments from people inside and outside the program and is asked to speak at numerous meetings. After the person speaks at a meeting, people tell him or her how much they got out of it. The person becomes a sponsor and soon has a flock of eager sponsees.

This is a variant of the know-it-all trap; it's easy to believe that we know all the answers. This is why we stress anonymity and humility. None of us knows all the answers, no matter how long we have been abstinent. We must always keep an open mind and remember that more will be revealed.

Another part of this trap is that our pride may make it difficult for us

---

[*]*Alcoholics Anonymous*, 89.

to ask for help when we need it. If we have problems—whether physical, emotional, or spiritual—we may be deluded into thinking it's not right for us to talk about them because we are supposed to be a strong inspiration for others.

We all have problems and we need to be able to talk openly and honestly about them. We need to let go of the pride that may keep us from wanting to go to meetings. I have met several onetime OA stars who ran into trouble and then made their relapse worse by allowing their pride to keep them from asking for help from other OA members.

❦ The emaciation trap

We live in a society where many people think you can't be too rich or too thin. After hitting goal weight, it's easy to delude ourselves into thinking that we need to lose another ten pounds. Even though I am now at goal weight, I still have some days when I look in the mirror and see a fat face staring back at me.

Another source of this I-should-lose-more-weight syndrome stems from the lasting body damage done by obesity. After we lose a lot of weight, our skin, which was stretched to hold all the fat, doesn't shrink as fast as the rest of our body, so we may have some loose skin. *Maybe it will go away if I lose another ten pounds* is a common thought. It doesn't. Exercise can help tone it up somewhat, but some of the damage never goes away.

Fear may cause you to want to dip below your goal weight. It's tempting when you are losing weight to want to lose additional pounds so that you can have a few "in the bank" in case you gain weight later.

Whatever the reason, becoming underweight is extremely dangerous. Tiredness, fatigue, and intolerance to cold are just a few of the side effects. Many women who lose too much weight stop menstruating. There is the danger that anorexia nervosa may develop. Indeed, many overeaters have flip-flopped between anorexia and overeating. If you become emaciated, your body will rebel and you may have severe cravings for food. These cravings are the legitimate warning signs of a starved body. And if you don't take care, it's easy to start eating compulsively again.

❦ The OA politics trap

Part of the OA tradition of anonymity is that we seek to place principles before personalities. Nevertheless, there are many opportunities in OA to place the personalities before the principles. That's what I call OA politics.

Problems can develop along this line: Because we know that our eating disorder is a life-and-death issue, we take this program very seriously. And we naturally think that our own viewpoint is right and that anyone who holds a different opinion is wrong. Therefore, since this is a life-and-death issue, those who are wrong are killing people. This can lead to some heated arguments. Over the years we have fought over everything from food plans to how to set up the chairs at meetings. Being human, we will continue to have our differences of opinion. Controversy seems to be a natural part of Anonymous programs, as you can see by reading a history of them, such as *AA Comes of Age*.

But if we get involved in personalities, we are doomed. OA politics gives us a lot of opportunities to practice our character defects and develop new ones. It's so easy to take the petty disputes personally and to develop resentments that explode into overeating.

People who do service for the sake of doing service get well. People who become OA politicians, out of pride or a need to control, may end up fat. As one cynic put it at a time when a local intergroup was raging with controversy, "To see recovery, go to a meeting; to see the disease, go to intergroup."

❦ Chasing newcomers

Some members are tempted to establish a sexual relationship with OA newcomers, which is sometimes called "Thirteenth-Stepping." This can severely hinder the recovery of both people. Oddly enough, the newcomer usually survives and the old-timer ends up overeating. An old-timer working a good program knows enough to keep his or her hands off newcomers. Thus, any old-timer who chases after newcomers is probably on shaky ground to begin with. When a relationship with a fellow program member goes well, it can go very well. But if it ends, there may be some natural resentments between the people. If they try to avoid each other by not going to OA meetings, the chances of relapse increase.

❦ Other distractions

As the weight comes off and our emotional well-being improves, we may get a tremendous desire to do the things we always said we would do if we lost the weight. We may jump into activities in that all-or-nothing way that addicts do. There may be a desire to sign up for night school, save the world, shop for a mate, and build our own house—all at once. But we need to remember to devote sufficient time to our recovery, or it won't last long.

I have found that when I put a lot of time into my OA program, abstinence is easy. When I cut back, abstinence becomes a struggle. Since I don't like to fight the food, the best way for me to stay abstinent is to put in the time. As I have heard at meetings, "You either put in the time or you put the food in your mouth."

One thing I need to remember is that there are only twenty-four hours in a day; I don't have time to do all the things that I want to do. Just as I must spend the dollars in my bank account to do me the most good, I must also spend my limited hours in the wisest manner.

The time involved in developing and maintaining relationships can also distract us from spending time on our recovery. Those who truly care about us, however, don't want us to suffer from compulsive overeating; even though they may not understand the program, they want us to do what we need to get well. Worthy community causes can also eat up a lot of time. Just remember that you can't help anyone if you kill yourself from overeating.

❦ The generics anonymous trap

A similar distraction can befall those who have more than one addiction and belong to other Anonymous programs in addition to OA. Those suffering from multiple addictions may soon find themselves going to several different programs and not making much progress in any because they don't have the time to work any one program thoroughly.

Some people have the false impression that one Anonymous program can substitute for any other. There are good reasons why there are separate programs for food, alcohol, drugs, and other problems. My observation is that the other Anonymous programs don't help very much with food. I recommend concentrating on one program at a time. To find out which one you should emphasize, ask yourself, "At the rate I am going now, what is going to kill me first?" Then concentrate on that one.

It's often recommended in OA that you wait until you have been abstinent for at least a year before exploring other Anonymous programs. They will take away from the time you need to put into recovering from overeating in that first year. Moreover, the other programs may stir up some intense feelings, so it's better to have some practice dealing with such feelings without overeating before you stir up more of them.

❦ OA underdose

It's hard to overdose on OA. Honest. Even if you put more time into the program than you have to, there are few adverse consequences. You may miss Monday Night Football one too many times, or your phone bill may be a bit higher than it otherwise would, but that's it. On the other hand, I have seen people die from underdoses of OA. What happens then is that you end up with a belly full of food and a head full of program, and that's really painful.

❦ The political correctness trap

This trap is related to the know-it-all trap. Some people have certain political beliefs that keep their minds closed and make them unwilling to work all the OA program. For example, some of us were "liberated" fat people who developed strong beliefs about our civil rights. We are upset over the unjust social and economic discrimination against fat people. Many of us wish to change the "Thin is beautiful" attitudes in our society and think that the emaciated look is absurd if not dangerous.

I agree with many of these points. Some OA members get caught in the cross fire between their own political view that fat is beautiful and their need to lose weight for medical reasons. A similar view is that attempting to lose weight means submitting to the tyranny of a sexist, male-dominated culture. Ask yourself, Do you want to be healthy and feel good about yourself, or do you want to be politically correct?

❦ The perfectionism trap

As addicts, we tend to be people who think and do things in extremes. If we can't be perfectly good, we have to be perfectly bad. This also manifests itself in our recovery. A common trap is to think that we have to be perfect—that one extra string bean means we have blown our abstinence so we might as well go out and binge. And if we're going to binge, we might as well do it right. If we can't be Mr. or Ms. OA, we can't show up at all.

That kind of diseased thinking will kill us. It's okay not to be perfect. We only have to be good enough. What we are seeking in OA is a sustainable way of living that keeps us from killing ourselves with excess food. Again, we don't have to be perfect, only good enough.

Perfectionism is a trap that overeaters fall into quite readily. We devote so much time and energy to a project that we can't keep up the pace. We may have a minor setback, get discouraged, and then give up. One of the beautiful things about being in OA is that we can be human, make mistakes, and still be welcome. We don't have to dress up to go to a meeting; we don't even have to be on time. Being late to a meeting is better than not showing up at all. Remember that there is a big difference between an overly large salad and a monster candy bar. Your program doesn't have to be perfect. I have yet to see anyone work a perfect program. If we were perfect, we wouldn't need OA in the first place.

Perfectionism is closely related to the star syndrome discussed earlier. Our pride makes us unable to admit our imperfections, so we become unwilling to talk about them. We may refuse to ask for help when we need it and thus guarantee trouble for ourselves.

Also closely related to the perfectionism trap is what I call the "binary thinking trap," in which we tend to make judgments that everything is either true or false, up or down, yes or no, recovered or bingeing, good or bad. We need to lighten up and recognize that there are a lot of gray areas in life.

❦ The sameness trap

Another common mistake is to think that all of us in the OA program are the same. Overeaters come in all shapes, sizes, creeds, and colors. Recall that the only requirement for membership is the desire to stop eating compulsively—and that covers a wide variety of eating disorders. It's sometimes said that one of the best things about OA is that we let anybody in; it's also said that one of the worst things about OA is that we let anybody in.

Failing to recognize this diversity can be a trap in two ways. First, you may be tempted to resent people who aren't like you, particularly if their eating disorder is different from your own. You may say things like, "What's he doing here? I'll bet he's never been fat." (You may be surprised.) Or if another person's food plan is different from what seems to be working for you, you may feel threatened. You may be confused if one person is able to eat foods that set off cravings in you. Or you may be eating a food that causes problems for someone else and wonder if that food will cause problems for you. Remember that there is a great deal of variety on the physical side of our disease. Some of us have different physical sensitivities, and getting upset over our differences won't do us any good. This is one of the reasons why many meetings discourage mentioning specific foods.

Second, modeling your recovery after someone whose eating disorder is different from yours may slow your own recovery. I have observed some who had suffered from morbid obesity listen to a dynamic speaker who had not suffered from morbid obesity. The eloquent speaker, who had an impressive recovery in his own way, talked about his notion that junk food was not addictive. The poor listeners, who failed to recognize that not everyone in OA suffers from a problem the same as their own, then thought that they could indeed eat anything and wound up reactivating their food addiction.

Relapse

A demoralizing feature of compulsive overeating is that there is always the danger of relapse. It's all too easy to get back into overeating with its attendant misery—the painful stuffed feelings, the food hangovers, the frightening sense of being out of control, the agony of not being able to fit into your clothes, the debilitation of obesity, the isolation, and the humiliation of being controlled by food. When we lost the weight, we were besieged with comments about how good we looked and how ugly we used to look. If we regain the weight, there is usually silence, except for the incessant voices in our own heads.

We have all been there. We have spent most of our lives in relapse.

Even after we come into OA, the threat of relapse doesn't go away; indeed, many people in OA have at least one relapse.

OA has a lot of experience with relapse, and we can learn from that experience how to prevent one and how to recover from one. Many of us have feared relapse. We know how painful the consequences of our overeating were and don't want to go back to them. Some of us, especially when we are still shaky in our brand-new abstinence, don't even want to hear about relapse because we fear that hearing about it will put us into one. It won't. Compulsive overeating isn't a communicable disease, so we don't have to be afraid to be around people in relapse.

❦ *Relapse warning signs*

As the old saying goes, an ounce of prevention is worth a pound of cure. Relapses don't strike out of the blue. It's not as if we walk down the street one day and suddenly get attacked by a jar of peanut butter lurking in the shadows. Warning signs usually alert us when we are in slippery places. Becoming aware of the warning signs is an important part of getting and staying better in OA; it's much easier to stay abstinent than to get abstinent.

Complacency is one warning sign of impending trouble. Our disease seems to go into hibernation from time to time, letting us think that we are cured. Or if we are knowledgeable enough to know that we aren't cured, the "stinking thinking" may tell us we can easily control our compulsion by ourselves. It's when we start to think that everything is fine with our program that we need to be extra watchful.

Unresolved anger is another poison that sidetracks many of us on our recovery journey. When our serenity is depleted by anger, that's a warning sign that the refrigerator isn't too far away. When we find ourselves in this condition, we need to redouble our spiritual efforts or else. In this situation, taking our inventory and praying are especially useful.

Closely related to unresolved anger is the absence of an "attitude of gratitude." We are often presented with situations where our glass may seem half empty rather than half full. But if we focus on what we don't have rather than being grateful for what we do have, we may be tempted to reward ourselves with food. Part of our emotional and spiritual recovery involves changing our attitude toward life so that we are grateful for what we have.

Failure to progress is another thing to watch for. Even those with long-term abstinence need to continue to work on their physical, emotional, and spiritual recovery. Once a sane eating pattern is established, there is still a lot of work involved in restructuring our lives to keep that eating sane. Some people stop at this point and do nothing more. They refuse to continue to work the Steps and refuse to do service at meetings. The results are as predictable as the tides. As the saying goes, "You can only coast downhill."

A drop in OA meeting attendance is such a major danger sign that it should set off alarm bells. When we stay away from meetings, we are no longer reminded about what we need to do to get better. What sometimes happens is that meeting attendance drops from several meetings a week, to once a week, and then once every several weeks. At the same time, the use of other program tools such as making telephone calls and reading the literature declines as well.

Often, the food stays reasonable for a while. This is where our disease is at its most cunning. It fools us into thinking that, yes indeed, we can get by without going to those stupid meetings.

☙ Anatomy of a relapse

As I've said, a relapse is preceded by a raft of warning signs that are often obvious to everyone except the endangered overeater. But if you try to warn an overeater in danger of relapse, you will often be met with a defensive reaction: "How dare you tell me I am not working my program properly! I have been abstaining for days/months/years and I know what I am doing. Why don't you take your own inventory instead?"

A person rarely goes directly from serene abstinence to severe, destructive binges. The pattern usually starts off with minor slips. Not every slip is the harbinger of a relapse, but when a person is vulnerable, that's how it usually starts. Some trivial excuse or special occasion comes along and there is a slip. And for the next few days, eating stays reasonable. This is where our tricky disease says to us "See! You are cured. Now you can eat junk food like normal people without having to binge!" But the food is patient.

Then, a few days or weeks go by and there is another slip. At this point, the disease has lulled us into thinking that it's no big deal and that we can control our eating whenever we want to. Many times I have heard people say at meetings that they took just one bite of a binge food and happily announced, "One bite doesn't mean a binge." Then a month later they were bingeing their brains out with unprecedented fury.

One of the first things to go, along with the food, is the clarity of thinking that proper eating brought to us. The mental fog returns and we actually believe some of the stupid rationalizations we tell ourselves. Our sense of self-esteem also suffers, because if we truly loved ourselves, why would we abuse our bodies with so much harmful food?

That sense of hopelessness returns. Relapsers often think, *I am just a hopeless overeater. Nothing, not even OA, will work for me. Why should I even bother?* Our disease tells us that we are hopeless, so we might as well eat.

Pride also gets in the way of recovery. We may become afraid about what others in the group will think of us after a relapse. We project our own food-induced judgmental attitude onto others. Sometimes the pride is so strong our disease will say to us, "I can't go to OA until I get my abstinence back." But OA is the place we need to go to get our abstinence back!

As the pounds creep on, the sense of desperation intensifies. Those stylish clothes we bought no longer fit. We struggle and struggle, trying to get back on the wagon, only to fall off again. We put together a few days or weeks of abstinence and then, wham, the food gets to us again and we are even more demoralized. Will this never end?

There is no telling how long a relapse will last. Some are short and some drag on for months and even years. Sooner or later it will end. This next section describes how to use some techniques that can make a relapse end sooner rather than later.

❦ *How to recover from a relapse*

At this point, I speak not from my own OA experience, but from the observations of others who have had relapses and recovered from them. If you are suffering from a relapse, find others who have been where you are and find out what they did to recover. Then do what they did. This is what I have seen work for others:

- Don't despair.
- Keep coming back.
- Ask for help.
- Find a relapse meeting.
- Talk to your sponsor.
- Use the tools of the program.
- Pray.
- Talk with other overeaters who have relapsed.
- Consider inpatient treatment.

Don't despair. The demoralization of a relapse is probably the most lethal part of it. Our disease says after a relapse that nothing will work for us, so we might as well eat. Remember that no one is perfect. We have all been through the wringer with food, and we all know how it feels to be knocked down again and again by the food. There is hope.

Other people who have had severe problems with relapse have recovered, and you can too. Your disease may tell you that OA won't work, and that you don't belong in OA because you can't stop overeating. Nonsense. Remember that the only requirement for OA membership is the desire—not the ability—to stop overeating compulsively.

Many have learned a lot from relapse. Although some cynics say that the only thing that we learn from a binge is how to binge, the truth is that many of us were not motivated to put any effort into OA until our food addiction beat us one more time. Relapse often opens up the willingness to grasp the entire program and all the benefits that come with it.

Keep coming back. A potentially fatal mistake you can make after a relapse is not to keep coming to meetings. It may be uncomfortable to sit at a meeting when you are stuffed and everyone is talking about how wonderful abstinence is, but at least it keeps you away from the refrigerator for a while. Even if you have to binge your way to and from meetings, at least keep going to them. The more meetings you go to, the better off you will be. Try to get to ninety OA meetings in ninety days. I have never seen anyone do that who didn't get abstinent sooner or later. At meetings, we will eventually hear what we need to get well.

Ask for help. Your pride may tell you that you can do it alone and that you don't need to tell anyone about your problems. But people can't help you if they don't know that you need help. Say at meetings that you are having problems and would like some support. Ask for people to call you. If you are feeling shaky, don't be afraid to ask for the company of another program member to help you get through some rough moments. There have been times when I let a person sleep on my sofa for the night because he or she felt shaky and worried about being able to make it through the night without eating. You may wish to ask another OA member to accompany you to the supermarket when you need to shop for food.

Find a relapse meeting. All over the country, special meetings are set up to discuss problems associated with relapse. Many I know who have recovered from relapse say that such meetings made them feel welcome when they felt uncomfortable at other meetings.

Talk to your sponsor. Find an abstinent person who is willing to work with you, like your sponsor. Then talk to that person every day. Keep in mind that you can change sponsors at any time. It's not a sponsor's job to run your life, only to share with you what worked for him or her.

Use the tools of the program. Although meetings and sponsorship are extremely useful, the other tools come in particularly handy after a relapse. A relapse often makes us willing to read such essentials as the Big Book thoroughly for the first time. And getting a service job at a meeting is a good way to ensure that you will get to a meeting when your disease is telling you to go to a bakery instead.

Pray. Prayer really works. It doesn't matter if you don't believe that it will work. Try it anyway and you will be amazed. Your prayers don't have to be eloquent masterpieces. Just try talking to God with any words that come to you.

Talk with other overeaters who have relapsed. Once again, remember that OA is a vast storehouse of experience, and that no matter what your problems, others within the fellowship have also had them. You can learn from those who have had similar problems, but first you must find them. That's why it's helpful to go to meetings and talk to people on the phone.

Consider inpatient treatment. Many fine inpatient facilities deal with eating disorders, and treatment at such a facility can accelerate your recovery, especially if you are having major problems. (Inpatient treatment will be discussed at length on p. 142.)

❧ *Working with others in relapse*

It's likely that over the years someone close to us will suffer from a relapse. Oftentimes our own fear of relapse makes it difficult to reach out to them, and many times we don't know what to do. Watching a relapse happen to someone close to us is almost as bad as suffering one ourselves. The best thing to do is to treat him or her the way we would like to be treated in the same situation.

When we are relatively new to the program, we don't know how to deal with people in relapse. We may be tempted to avoid them, which is the worst possible response. Now, more than ever, those having trouble with food need love and support. Calling them from time to time lets them know that we care, that our feelings for them aren't based on what they ate today. Offering to give them a ride to a meeting can be of tremendous benefit. It ensures that we and they will get to meetings, and it makes a binge on the way home much less likely.

Try to recall what it was like in your bingeing days and then put yourself in their shoes. A person in relapse is already feeling pretty bad and does not need any help in feeling worse.

It's often tempting to give unsolicited advice: Go to OA meetings. Get a sponsor. Eat this way. But a person in relapse has already heard all this and knows what to do. The problem isn't about knowledge, but willingness. If we give unsolicited advice, we will sound like all the controlling people who have been telling overeaters to go on diets. On the other hand, it's easy to go to the other extreme and act, out of a misguided sense of love, as a nursemaid during binges and participate in the denial of the relapse. We may validate their excuses for eating with "Oh poor baby, no wonder you ate. . . ."

In Step One, we admitted that we were powerless over food. This means not only our own food, but that of others as well. We can't control how others eat, no matter how hard we try. We carry the message, not the person. We need to take care of our own recovery and not get bent out of shape by trying to fix others. Often, a little dose of Al-Anon comes in handy. What I try to do around friends who are having problems isn't lecture but instead show my concern by phoning them and greeting them at meetings. A bit of affection, such as a hug or a neck rub, means a lot. I try not to give advice unless asked, and I try to stick to my own experience: This is how I got abstinent, This is what I did, This is what I have observed, and so on. And, of course, I don't forget to include them in my prayers.

Inpatient treatment

In the last few years, there has been a tremendous growth of inpatient hospital programs that treat eating disorders. They are known as Eating Disorder Units, or EDUs. This is long overdue. A good inpatient program can benefit anyone who is really struggling with food, whether a newcomer to OA or an old-timer suffering from relapse.

In the early days of Alcoholics Anonymous, it was virtually a requirement that new members be hospitalized before joining a group. Early AA members realized the benefits of taking newly sober people out of their old environment. It gave them time to concentrate on their recovery without interference from their families, jobs, and old drinking buddies.

AA has a long history of successful cooperation with hospitals and alcohol rehabilitation centers. Virtually every chemical dependency rehabilitation center believes that regular AA attendance is the best way to keep its patients from relapsing. And the best EDUs realize that introducing their patients to OA and encouraging regular meeting attendance during and after hospitalization greatly increase the success rate of the EDU. A few EDUs have the mistaken impression that OA is trying to compete with them for patients. We aren't. We try to cooperate with hospitals as much as possible by establishing meetings in those hospitals and making sure that patients have meeting schedules.

Eating disorder inpatient programs usually last at least four weeks and are expensive, but if you can afford it, the good ones are worth it. They will provide you with a safe environment away from the refrigerator where you can start your recovery.

The quality of inpatient treatment varies widely. Since attending one is time-consuming and expensive, check it out carefully. Talk to other OA members who have been through inpatient treatment to see what they recommend. Then, call several different treatment centers and ask to talk to some of their former patients. Here are eight questions to ask about each treatment center.

1. *How long have they been treating eating disorders and how many patients have they treated?* Obviously, you will prefer a place that has been in business longer and has more experience. Some hospitals have a long history of treating chemical dependency and are very good at it, but they have only recently opened an EDU to fill empty hospital beds and cash in on a growing market.

2. *What is the mix of patients (age, sex, and type of eating disorder)?* One thing to watch out for is the mix of patients in the EDU. Some treatment centers mix the morbidly obese with purgers who have never been fat and anorexics who have never purged. I believe this isn't the best way, since the three groups are very different. Sometimes the ratios between these groups become quite unbalanced. I once visited an EDU where the patient population that week consisted of fifteen female teenage bulimarexics, one extremely obese boy, and one fifty-year-old three-hundred-pound woman. To me, this didn't seem like an effective mix for treatment.

3. *What is the staff's experience?* Find out what kind of experience the staff has and try to talk to the treatment staff (not the marketing department) before you make your decision. How long have they been doing this? What kind of credentials do they have? Are they recovering overeaters themselves? If so, do they have the kind of recovery that you want?

4. *What does the treatment consist of?* Treatment philosophies vary considerably from treatment center to treatment center, so find out what you will be doing during your stay. Some places are little more than glorified fat farms with diet and exercise regimes; others use intense psychotherapy. Even the philosophies on nutrition vary substantially. The better treatment centers encourage OA participation by taking patients to meetings during treatment and encouraging regular meeting attendance after the patient leaves. This helps the patient get accustomed to OA before he or she is discharged, and it helps the EDU by increasing its visibility among people with eating disorders. Word of mouth within the fellowship is a great marketing tool for EDUs.

5. *Where is it?* Although a treatment center closer to home is more convenient, you may wish to travel further to go to a place with an established reputation. The travel expenses to a further location are a small fraction of the total time and money you are investing.

6. *How successful is the treatment program?* Find out the long-term success rate of the program you are considering, but don't be surprised if reliable numbers are unavailable. It's hard to keep track of people years later to see how they are doing. Ask questions such as the following: How many patients are still purge-free one year after discharge? How many patients continue to lose weight after discharge? How many patients are keeping that weight off one, two, and five years down the road? Be aware that the numbers may be exaggerated. The successful patients will keep in touch with the hospital while the ones who have regained the weight back may be too embarrassed to reply to follow-up surveys.

7. *What kind of aftercare is provided?* Some units provide aftercare on an ongoing basis; others provide group therapy or individual sessions with counselors. Find out what is included, how much it costs, and how long it lasts. Talk to some of the alumni to find out how useful they have found it.

8. *How much does it cost, and will my insurance pay for it?* Inpatient treatment for an eating disorder is expensive, and getting one's insurance company to pay for it can be tricky. Most insurance companies don't pay for weight-loss treatments. They have seen enough quack cures over the years, so they are justifiably skeptical. Although they are well aware that morbidly obese patients run up more than their share of medical expenses, insurance companies don't want to pay for treatment after which clients regain all their weight. But most of the better health plans do have a variety of mental health benefits that can be used to pay for treatment. If you are seriously considering hospitalization, talk to the staff of the EDU to see whether or not your insurance will cover treatment.

Many insurance plans cover hospitalization for severe depression. Since depression and overeating are often interrelated, it may be possible to get the insurance company to pay under a diagnosis of depression. Many also cover treatment for bulimia. Even if you have never vomited, you may still qualify as a bulimic. Following are the technical diagnostic criteria for bulimia nervosa adopted by the American Psychiatric Association:[*]

- Recurrent episodes of binge-eating (rapid consumption of a large amount of food in a discrete period of time).
- A feeling of lack of control over eating behavior during the eating binges.
- Regularly engaging in one or more of the following in order to prevent weight gain: self-induced vomiting, use of laxatives or diuretics, strict dieting or fasting, or vigorous exercise.
- A minimum average of two binge-eating episodes a week for at least three months.
- Persistent overconcern with body shape and weight.

Does that sound familiar? Note that purging isn't required for a diagnosis of bulimia; obsessive dieting or fasting to control weight also counts. I believe that most OA members technically qualify as bulimics.

---

[*] *Diagnostic and Statistical Manual for Mental Disorders,* 3d. ed., revised (DSM-III-R) (Washington, D.C.: American Psychiatric Asociation, 1987), 167.

More on sponsorship

Helping other overeaters is an important part of getting better in OA. When we reach out and try to teach someone else what has worked for us, it reinforces what we need to do to hold on to our own recovery. By attempting to pass recovery on to others, we progress further in our own. It's also a lot of fun and a joy to participate in the recovery of others.

No method of sponsorship is the right method for every person. Individual style is also involved. This goes for the sponsor and the person being sponsored. Some people want to be told what to do; others rebel if anyone tells them what to do. Sometimes a person needs a shoulder to cry on; other times a person needs a kick in the pants. It takes judgment and experience to know what is needed.

The primary job of a sponsor isn't to tell other people what to do, but to share what works. Your experience in recovery is what you are sharing. Remember that the people you sponsor are doing more for you than you are for them.

And unless you are licensed to practice law, psychiatry, or medicine, don't. Even those who are professionals find that it's best for them not to mix their profession with sponsorship. But don't be afraid to recommend professional assistance when you feel that a sponsee could benefit from it; you aren't expected to be all things to all people.

❦ *When to start sponsoring*

OA doesn't have a certification process for sponsors, so you may not know when you are ready to start sponsoring. I suggest that you have at least three months in OA, have read the AA Big Book, and have started to work the Twelve Steps. I don't recommend trying to sponsor others if you are having problems with food. After all, you can't share what you haven't got, and the food may harm your judgment.

Two other signs indicate that you are ready to sponsor: (1) when your own sponsor suggests it, and (2) when others ask you to sponsor them.

Unfortunately, many people hesitate too long before they start sponsoring because they are afraid that they don't know how to do it. You don't have to—nor are you expected to—know all the answers. It's okay to say "I don't know." If you are presented with a situation that you don't know how to handle, say, "Let me get back to you on that one," and then ask your own sponsor or other OA members for their suggestions.

Keep in mind that, in general, you are able to sponsor up to the level of your own recovery. You may not feel that you have come far or have much to offer, but let your sponsee be the judge of that and not you. You may not realize how far you have progressed until you work closely with someone who is just like you once were. You don't have to achieve some mystic enlightenment or even goal weight to start sponsoring.

It may sound strange, but being a sponsor will help you as much as or more than it helps your sponsee. To get better, you should start sponsoring as soon as you are able.

❦ Where to find people to sponsor

The easiest place to find people to sponsor is at an OA meeting. People who come to OA meetings are there because they need help with their eating disorder. Many meetings ask those who are available to sponsor others to identify themselves. Just stand up and say that you are available. If you keep doing this, eventually you will have plenty of people to sponsor.

Also, feel free to greet newcomers and offer to help them get started if they are looking for a sponsor. I was helped tremendously at my first meeting by a kind person who did that for me. It's easy to help a newcomer because the questions they ask are usually simple and easy to answer.

Remember that you don't have to agree to sponsor every person who asks you. But if you decline a request to sponsor someone, do it very gently. It takes a lot of courage to ask for a sponsor and the fear of rejection is great. Whenever I have to turn someone down, I usually offer to be a temporary sponsor until he or she can find a permanent one.

Here are five reasons to turn someone down:

- *A full load.* You aren't doing yourself or the people you sponsor any favors if you spread yourself too thin by trying to sponsor too many people. They won't get the attention they deserve and you will feel rushed and overburdened. You will start resenting their calls when in fact they are helping you more than you are helping them.
- *Wrong gender.* It's an old tradition in Twelve Step programs to sponsor people of the same sex. We usually understand our own sex better, and there is less chance of a jealous spouse or a messy romantic entanglement to derail our recovery. But this tradition isn't etched in stone, and sometimes there are good reasons to sponsor someone, or have a sponsor, of the opposite sex. Two of my best sponsors, including the one who saved my life, have been female. At some OA meetings, there are few men, so it's necessary for some women to sponsor men.
- *Unwillingness.* If you feel that someone isn't yet willing to work the program, it's okay not to waste your time on him or her. Before I agree to sponsor people, I find out if they are willing to put in the time to go to a lot of OA meetings. If they aren't, then I figure that they aren't ready to recover yet, and that it would be dishonest of me to pretend that they can get better without their doing the work I believe

is essential. The time that you devote to someone who is unwilling to work the program could better be spent on someone who is.

- *Lack of an eating disorder.* Occasionally, but rarely, you will find someone who wanders into OA who really doesn't suffer from an eating disorder. He or she may be emotionally disturbed or just lonely. More likely, such a person is a victim of the modern preoccupation with weight.
- *Lack of similar experience.* In OA, you will find people with every type of eating disorder imaginable. It makes sense that your experience can best be put to work helping others like yourself. My own experience has been in recovering from severe, intractable, chronic obesity, and I sponsor other men who, like me, have been severely obese.

❦ Getting started

I agree with my sponsee to arrange a time each day to talk on the phone. I have found that brief daily contact is most helpful. It's frustrating to have a sponsor you can't get in touch with when you need him or her.

In our daily calls, my sponsees and I talk about all parts of the OA program. I don't believe in having one sponsor for food and another for the Steps the way some people do. I believe that in order to recover we must deal with all parts of the program and that a sponsor needs to guide sponsees in all areas, up to the level of their own recovery. Some sponsors give daily reading and writing assignments to the people they sponsor, but I have never done so.

Since it's helpful for newcomers to discuss what they are eating, I encourage this but don't require it. I help them to plan in advance what they are going to eat each day and to tell me, because this is what I did and it worked for me. It made me more likely to stick to what I committed to, and it was a tremendous help in making sure that my planned meals were defrosted in time to eat.

I really don't care what style of eating or food plan my sponsees choose, as long as it works for them. I know that I have changed food plans many times over the years and that I reserve the right to change my food plan at any time. I figure that if they are going to a lot of OA meetings and working the rest of the program, eventually they will settle on a style of eating that works for them.

Nor do I care if they eat foods that I don't eat, as long as they are healthy ones. I don't pretend that we are all the same in OA and that we should eat the same things. There is much that we don't know about appropriate nutrition for people with eating disorders, and we need to allow experimentation so that each of us can find what works. But I do make it clear that eating junk food isn't the path to recovery.

One thing I also emphasize, especially with newcomers, is using the tools of the program. The tools are the way we put the Twelve Steps into action. I monitor a sponsee's progress in all eight of the tools—abstinence, meetings, phone calls, service, sponsorship, anonymity, writing, and literature. Usually, I don't have to say too much about them. Just asking where a sponsee is with respect to each tool is a strong enough suggestion to use them.

I make sure that they are reading the program literature, including the AA Big Book. One useful exercise in reading the Big Book is to underline the words "must," "have to," or "require." They appear many times and point out the really important parts of the program.

I also suggest that they get a service job as soon as possible, such as setting up the literature at a meeting. Doing service makes newcomers feel included and helps the weight come off faster. I feel so strongly about the benefits of service that I won't sponsor people unless they are willing to do some form of service. If they aren't willing to do something so simple as setting up literature at meetings, I doubt that they will be willing to take the more difficult actions needed to work the Steps and recover.

Often, sponsees want specific advice about food. It's certainly okay to share what does and doesn't work for you—that's part of your job. But sometimes they may want you to make all their decisions for them. Don't fall into this trap. Make it clear that you aren't trained as a professional dietitian and that they must take responsibility for what they eat.

Sponsees also often have questions about the nutritional adequacy of their food plans. It's amazing to me how we who lived on junk food for months at a time suddenly start to worry about whether our food plan has enough fiber! I recommend that all my sponsees do a complete nutritional analysis of their food from time to time. Finding a book on nutrition and analyzing what you are eating is a wonderful educational exercise. By adding up the nutrients you are getting in your food plan and comparing them to the recommended dietary allowances, you can see if you are getting enough of what you need. You can also compare the total number of calories you are getting from protein, carbohydrates, and fat to make sure there isn't too much fat in your food plan. This exercise teaches you the nutritional content of the foods in your food plan and tells you whether they are meeting your body's needs. A professional nutritionist can do this for you too. Or you can buy special computer software that allows you to do this on many personal computers.

❧ Getting into the Steps

When a sponsee has finished reading the Big Book and *The Twelve Steps and Twelve Traditions of Overeaters Anonymous,* he or she is usually ready to start working the Steps more formally. The first action I recommend is to memorize the Twelve Steps. I am amazed at the number of people in OA who pay lip service to working the Steps but who don't really know what they are. Memorizing the Steps makes them a stronger part of our lives.

I usually discuss each Step during our daily calls. I share how I handled various problems and what other people have done in similar situations. When a sponsee is ready to take each Step, it's useful to have him or her state each Step formally. For example, "I am powerless over food and my life has become unmanageable."

When it comes to writing out the personal inventory for the Fourth Step, I make it clear to my sponsees that they don't have to read the inventory to me if they don't want to. This is so they can be as fearless and thorough as possible without editing it for me.

Some sponsors suggest that their sponsees do written exercises for each Step. The only Step that I believe has to be written is the personal inventory in Step Four, although written Tenth Step inventories are also useful.

Over the years, people will ask you to listen to their Fifth Step. It's an honor to be asked, as well as a great responsibility. Everything you hear must be treated with the strictest confidentiality. Remember, too, that those taking this Step are likely to be nervous and afraid of how you will react to some of their revelations. Do your best to put them at ease.

Sometimes you will be asked to listen to a Fourth Step that's extremely long. In those situations, I ask the person to prepare a one-or two-page summary listing the major problems. Then we start with the summary so that the most important areas are covered even if we don't have time to read all the other pages.

When you listen to someone else's inventory, remember that it's not your job to solve that person's problems. Don't play therapist. Act like a concerned friend. Listen carefully to what the person says, and if you wish, put him or her at ease by sharing some of your own experiences. You aren't expected to give advice, but helpful suggestions are sometimes appreciated.

I also recommend to my sponsees that they start sponsoring as soon as possible. I know how much sponsoring other overeaters has kept me going and improved the quality of my own recovery.

❧ Helping with food problems

It's more than likely that your sponsee will occasionally have problems with food. These problems may range from wanting to overeat, to minor deviations from planned meals, to minor slips, to major binges. Remember that we are human and that we make mistakes. The simplest way of dealing with these situations is to treat your sponsee the way you would like to be treated in the same situation.

The pain of overeating is punishment enough; you don't need to add to your sponsee's problems. Your sponsee may be discouraged and ready to give up altogether, or may be afraid that you will get angry and refuse to work with him or her anymore. You need to reassure your sponsee that you will continue your sponsoring relationship as long as necessary. The fact that your sponsee is having trouble means that he or she needs good sponsorship even more.

After I had been in OA for about two weeks, I had a minor slip. I was out of town on a business trip and I added some items to my dinner that didn't belong there. The next morning when I called my sponsor, I was gripped with fear. Should I tell him? What would he say? I thought I had blown it and was going to fail. I was afraid he would yell at me like some insensitive clod.

He didn't yell. He didn't lecture. He didn't say, "Oh you poor thing." All he said was, "What are you going to do about it?" It was a calm, reassuring, and friendly but businesslike approach. That's what I recommend when problems arise. Be calm, reassuring, and friendly, but businesslike. After talking with me regularly, my sponsees know what they need to do, so they don't need a lecture. I avoid giving specific advice unless asked.

☙ Letting go

Let go of the results of your sponsoring. No matter how hard you try, or how brilliant your words are, some people you sponsor will get well in spite of you. Remember that you came to OA because you were powerless over food. Not only are you powerless over your own food, but you are also powerless over the food of others.

Some people you sponsor will recover so quickly that it will be amazing. A few of them will never get well. Some will have heartbreaking relapses. Several will ask you to sponsor them and then never call. Sometimes I get frustrated and think I am a lousy sponsor when my sponsees don't get a certain part of the program. Then I am encouraged by the stories of the AA founders. When they wrote that helping others was the "foundation stone" of their recovery, they didn't mean hanging around at meetings with guys who had been sober for thirty years.[*] They meant working with people who, for all practical purposes, were still reeking of booze, many of whom didn't make it. Knowing that it's my reaching out that matters, not the results, helps keep me going.

☙ Ending a sponsor/sponsee relationship

Sooner or later the sponsor/sponsee relationship ends, although sometimes it can last for years. There are many reasons for the relationship to end. Life

---

[*] *Alcoholics Anonymous*, 97.

circumstances may change or one may move away. Sometimes a sponsee learns as much as possible from one person and feels it's time to move on. Your pride may be hurt, but remember not to take it personally; your sponsee has done you a service by allowing you to carry the message. Now you need to find someone else to help in order to hold on to your own recovery.

Occasionally, you may find yourself in a situation that doesn't seem to be working out and you may feel unable to sponsor someone any longer. Suppose you are sponsoring someone of the opposite sex and you suspect that romantic feelings are coming up. Getting romantically involved with a person you are sponsoring is a gross violation of trust and everything the program stands for. If you must step down as someone's sponsor, do it as gently as possible. Don't make it an abrupt termination. Give the person advance warning instead so he or she has plenty of time to look for a new sponsor.

What happens far more often is that your sponsee will drop you first. That's no big deal. Most sponsoring relationships are temporary, and there comes a time when a person feels ready to move on. Some just stop calling; others will call to tell you that they are ready for another sponsor. I feel that sponsors are a lot like teachers—we learn what we can from one and then move on to another.

I have occasionally heard horror stories about a sponsor firing his or her sponsee because the sponsee was having problems with food. I think the practice is deplorable and demonstrates the sponsor's severe misunderstanding of the program. An overeater who is in trouble needs a sponsor more than ever. The mere fact that a sponsee is willing to keep calling is evidence of a willingness to get well. As long as a sponsee is willing to keep calling me regularly, I will continue to sponsor him or her as long as necessary, no matter how much trouble he or she is having with food.

To those who care

If you care about someone with an eating disorder, keep in mind that unless you too have an eating disorder, you probably don't know what it's like. If your desire for food naturally coincides with your body's need for food, you should be grateful. It's difficult to convey what having an eating disorder is like. To an overeater, eating too much food is the most natural thing in the world. For some unknown reason, our brains send us signals to eat too much. You may have been bewildered at why we ate so much. You aren't alone; we were bewildered as well.

You have been through a lot. Watching us gain and lose weight, binge and starve, may have made you cynical about our chances of getting better. You have watched us try many crazy diet schemes, and you may think OA is just another one that will eventually fade away. Your skepticism is understandable. But OA treats the problem of compulsive overeating from a different perspective than diets. It sees obesity merely as the symptom of an eating disorder and believes that a fundamental change in the way we live our lives is necessary to achieve lasting relief.

Perhaps you are blaming part of our eating problems on yourself. They aren't your fault. Overeaters, like other addicts, may try to blame others for their behavior. They may say things like "If only you hadn't said this, I wouldn't have to eat." Or, "If you hadn't baked that, I wouldn't have to eat." No one really knows what causes eating disorders, but strong evidence now indicates a genetic connection. An effective cure is a long way off. This means that we overeaters are locked into a difficult long-term struggle, and that our problems won't magically disappear after we lose the weight. That's why we continue to attend meetings long after we reach our desired weight. Indeed, attending OA meetings is one of the most important things we do to maintain our weight reduction and our sanity.

Even though you haven't caused us to develop an eating disorder, and you can't force us to get better, chances are that being around people like us has caused you to develop some problems of your own. In the addiction field, there is much discussion about *codependency*—a disorder in which those who are affected by the addict's behavior sometimes become overly concerned, if not obsessed, with controlling that person's behavior. A codependent may also aid the addiction by participating in the addict's denial. For example, you might say, "What! The doctor told you to lose a hundred pounds! The nerve! You may be a bit plump, but you aren't that fat!" Often, codependents will vacillate between aiding the addict's denial and nagging the addict to do something about his or her eating.

The codependent may get several emotional payoffs from this relationship. For example, the codependent may derive a sense of superiority from not engaging in the excesses of the addict. The addict then becomes the identified "patient" and the codependent can focus attention on that person's problems instead of his or her own. The codependent may also use the addict's overeating as a bargaining tool to get the addict to do or accept things that he or she wouldn't otherwise.

The codependent may also be an addict. One classic combination is that of an alcoholic married to a compulsive overeater—she puts up with his drinking and he tolerates her overeating or vice versa.

It would be nice if there were a program like Al-Anon for those close to overeaters. Al-Anon is the classic program for those who are affected by another's alcoholism. It was started by the spouses of the AA founders, and it uses the AA principles to help the friends and families of alcoholics. It's a good place to learn about addiction and relationships with addicts.

Instead of focusing on how to get the addict to stop using, Al- Anon helps those living with an addict to focus on how to help themselves. This can be a real lifesaver.

Unfortunately, there is no strong counterpart for OA. Some people have started up O-Anon meetings for the families and friends of compulsive overeaters, but O-Anon meetings are few and far between and haven't thrived. For friends and family who are bothered by the overeating of someone else and are curious about how to deal with it, I recommend trying some Al-Anon meetings. What follows is advice specifically addressed to the parents and partners of overeaters, but a lot of the advice is useful for anyone who wants to help an overeater.

❦ To parents

I am only a new parent, so my comments are based on my experience growing up as a fat kid. Watching a child struggle with all the problems of being fat must be very painful. Having your hopes raised by a brief stint of successful dieting, only to see them dashed when the weight is regained, is a sickening feeling for you and your child. You must be bewildered about why your child can't control his or her eating. Your child is bewildered too. Your struggle to control your child's weight and eating may lead to bitter family arguments. More often, it teaches your child to be a secret eater.

It's popular now to blame parents for everything that goes wrong, and your child has probably already blamed you. I know I would complain to my mother for feeding me too much, but then ask her to make a batch of fudge. No wonder she was confused. But it's not all your fault. Chances are, very little of it's your fault. Studies of adopted children indicate that obesity tends to be inherited from the biological parents, regardless of who raises the children. If children don't have the genes that predispose them to obesity, there is nothing you can do to make them obese.

Overweight children aren't stupid. You may be unconsciously influenced by our culture's unwarranted prejudices against fat people. If you ask why your child broke his or her diet, you may be appalled by the idiotic excuses you get, but that doesn't mean he or she is unintelligent. (Witness the imaginative ways your child manages to get food.) Your child has an eating disorder, but he or she can live a full life despite the problem.

Choices for handling your child's obesity. As a parent, you have some options: (1) You can ignore the problem and hope that it goes away. This actually happens more than you might think.[*] Assure your child that you

---

[*]National Research Council, *Diet and Health* (Washington D.C., 1989), 582. (The National Research Council reports that the risk of a fat child becoming a fat adult is far less than many people think. Studies show that remission occurs in a large percentage of overweight children.)

will love him or her no matter what. Support your child in any way he or she needs. (2) You can yell at your child for being fat and make nasty comments every time he or she eats something fattening. This doesn't work, and your child will justifiably hate you for being abusive.

The usual approach is to drag the child to diet doctors, shrinks, commercial diet clubs, and so forth. These are good ways to waste money and reinforce in your child the notion that he or she is lovable only if he or she loses weight. I am not knocking doctors or therapists. Most of them sincerely try to help their patients, but you can't force an unwilling child to get better. Children in this situation will often say and do things to please their parents, even though deep in their hearts they feel the effort is useless.

This can begin the yo-yo syndrome that so many overeaters have been on. We would lose ten pounds, then gain twenty, lose twenty, then gain thirty, and so on. By the time we became adults, the weight fluctuations became fifty- and hundred-pound tidal waves. Each time we dieted, we taught our bodies that food was scarce and that we had to store up every calorie we could for the next famine. I am convinced that many people would never have had a serious weight problem if they hadn't harmed their bodies with years of crazy dieting. If they had just learned to accept those ten extra pounds when they were fourteen, I believe they wouldn't have had to fight the fifty extra pounds when they were thirty.

Strange as it may seem, *not* making an issue of the weight may be the best approach, especially if your child isn't extremely obese. Some children do grow out of it. And making your child's weight a major issue leads to a variety of problems. For example, if your child is forced to diet, he or she will learn to be a sneak eater. If you withhold approval because your child is fat, it magnifies the stigma that the rest of society places on obese people. Your child needs all the love and support he or she can get. Putting extreme emphasis on your child's weight creates a fertile environment for compulsive overeating that can lead to bulimia or anorexia.

Children are exposed to the societal madness over weight at an early age. Television and magazines teach them that fat is ugly and unacceptable. Some fear becoming fat more than they fear a nuclear holocaust. Large numbers of them start dieting because their classmates diet; they see that the way to get approval is to lose weight, even if there are no medical reasons for them to do so. Some children starve themselves to the point of danger and become anorexic. Anorexia is a severe eating disorder with a high mortality rate. If you suspect your child is anorexic, I urge you to seek professional advice immediately.

Many young overeaters fast, exercise compulsively, use laxatives, or vomit to avoid the results of their overeating. If you suspect your child of such behavior, be very concerned. Some young people flirt with vomiting for a while and then give it up when they realize how dangerous it is. Part of this is the generally reckless behavior of youth, which most children outgrow. But those who can't stop are truly bulimic. If your child is bulimic, get professional advice on the best treatment available, and don't hesitate to recommend OA.

In addition to starting the yo-yo syndrome, diets can also stunt your child's growth, especially if your child is at an age where he or she should be having a growth spurt. I believe that one of the reasons I didn't grow to be as tall as my father is that I dieted when I should have been growing. That, plus eating too much junk food at other times, probably caused permanent damage.

The best thing to do. Set a good example. Kids automatically imitate their parents. If you eat the right foods in the right amounts, they will learn from your example. They may not be as skinny as the fashion of the day dictates, but they won't be nearly as fat as they could be if they had learned bad eating habits at home.

I also don't condone feeding children junk food. Children naturally love candy and they quickly learn how to get it on their own, so you don't have to go out of your way to get it for them. Parents don't show love for their children by feeding them empty calories. Junk food displaces nutritious food and thus deprives children of needed nutrients. Teaching your child poor nutrition habits is a form of child abuse.

Forcing overweight children to eat differently than the rest of the family will make them feel unloved and resentful. For example, a young child may not comprehend why the rest of the family gets dessert and he or she doesn't. Instead, I recommend setting a good example by feeding the entire family the same nutritious food.

Notice that I haven't suggested you drag an overweight child to OA, although you may want to suggest it when the child is old enough. I haven't seen much in the way of recovery for young children. To recover in OA, a person needs to be mature enough to understand the cause-and-effect relationship between overeating and gaining weight, as well as be able to comprehend that he or she has a problem with overeating, not just extra weight. Few youngsters have reached the level of desperation necessary to grasp the OA program. If a child doesn't yet have the desire to stop eating compulsively, he or she won't get anything out of OA, and this desire isn't something parents can force.

Being old enough to go to meetings independently is also helpful. Although OA has no age requirements, my impression is that young people who recover in OA are at least in their late teens.

❦ To the mate

Living with a compulsive overeater, even a recovering one, can be very frustrating. Watching someone you love be defeated by food time after time is painful. You are probably baffled by the behavior. You know that the obesity is life-threatening, and yet he or she continues to eat. You want to ask, *Why if you have been on a diet for so long is your weight still going up? Why did you regain all the weight it took you so long to lose? Why are you eating foods that you know aggravate your diabetes? Don't you love me enough to stop doing that?*

Don't bother asking these questions; your mate probably doesn't know the answers. There are many theories about why people overeat and many have some validity, but we really don't know why. It hasn't been determined yet. Even if someone does figure it out, knowing what caused it isn't necessarily going to make it stop.

Be honest with yourself. Make sure you are honest with yourself. Do you want your mate to be fat? Do you feel insecure and fear that your mate will lose weight and then run off and leave you? Obesity changes the balance of power in a relationship. Many overeaters are so incapacitated by their fat, both physically and emotionally, that they became dependent on those around them. You may resent this dependence but also enjoy the power and control it gives you. Remember that compulsive overeating is slowly but relentlessly killing your mate, one bite at a time. Before the body gives out, there are years, if not decades, of progressively worse incapacitation, humiliation, and pain.

Many times, overeaters get mixed messages from those who love them: "The doctor says if you don't lose that weight you're going to have a stroke." Then, "Here, have another cookie." Still, your mate's overeating isn't your fault. Although your mate may accuse you of all kinds of nasty things, you didn't force-feed him or her. Your mate picked up the fork and likewise must put it down.

Don't try to control your mate's eating. That will just make him or her resentful and sneaky. But you don't have to finance or otherwise enable binges. Your mate knows how to get food and can get it without your help. Refusing to assist in activities harmful to your mate's health isn't an act of defiance but an act of love. And if you value your life, don't try to get between an overeater and his or her food. I once met a woman in OA who stabbed her husband with her fork because he kept taking food off her plate.

Don't nag. Nagging will create nothing but pain for both of you. Your mate knows that he or she is fat, and knows that overeating will make him or her fatter, and still can't stop. Verbal abuse won't help. It will only lead to resentments that will make it even more difficult for your mate to recover.

What then can you do to help your mate? First of all, you don't have to aid in the denial. When your mate's overeating comes up, tell the truth without nagging. If he or she doesn't seem interested in doing anything about the problem, there is little you can do about it. But if your mate seems to want to do something about it, you may wish to broach the subject of OA with this book in hand. Offer to watch the kids while he or she tries a few meetings.

Becoming obsessed with trying to fix your mate is a good recipe for making yourself crazy. You may find help for yourself in Al-Anon meetings. By learning to detach with love from your mate's eating disorder and working on your own serenity and peace of mind, you will make it easier for your mate to recover by reducing the stress level in the family.

One thing you may wish to consider is planning an intervention. This is done when the family and friends confront the addict in an attempt to break down the denial and induce him or her to accept treatment. If you are considering such a move, you should consult with a therapist who has intervention experience.

If your mate does join OA, you can expect him or her to go through many changes as the recovery process begins. During some of these changes, your mate may be temporarily even harder to live with than when he or she was overeating. For example, during the withdrawal phase your mate will feel tired, irritable, and grouchy. Fortunately, this passes rather quickly. Sometimes he or she may act holier-than-thou and look down on those who still eat junk food; other times your mate may be busy with OA activities and you may feel neglected. But remember that the many benefits of recovery are worth it. Your mate will be healthier not only physically, but emotionally, and will have greater serenity and peace of mind that will more than make up for the difficult times.

Cooperate with each other about food. Here is a point that will make your life together a little more harmonious: Make sure you cooperate in seeing that your mate eats on time. Since most overeaters in recovery don't snack between meals, a delayed meal means that we can become hungry and irritable. Although most people can have "just a little something" to tide them over, that can be dangerous for a recovering overeater because it can lead to nonstop eating.

Overeaters are sometimes demanding about the foods they want and throw temper tantrums if they can't get exactly what they want. They sometimes feel that the rest of the world owes them something because they stopped abusing themselves with food. Fortunately, as they continue to grow, they learn to deal with their families in a more mature way and such tantrums cease.

The best thing you can do is to be supportive, to let your mate know you love him or her no matter what. Don't complain if your mate spends a lot of time at OA meetings. It's the best place for an overeater to be. If it were possible to recover from overeating without putting in so much time, overeaters would have done it long ago. Usually, by the time an overeater reaches OA, all other remedies have been tried. For overeaters, OA is literally do or die.

❦ To doctors

I am not a medical doctor and won't presume to tell doctors how to do their jobs. But I will try to give some additional insight and understanding that doctors can use to be more effective with their patients who are overeaters.

We overeaters have been lousy patients and we know it. Most of us know the risks of being overweight. We can probably recite verbatim the infamous lecture we have heard so many times. Many of us have already suffered a lot of the physical effects of obesity, such as stretch marks, hypertension, diabetes, joint problems, and heart disease. We knew that our obesity was killing us, and still we couldn't stop eating.

We have come desperately to you for help, begging for a cure for our problems. You tried everything—diets, pills, shots, supervised fasts, surgery—and still we ate. It must have been very frustrating for you to see such pain and despair, so much morbidity and mortality, to try so hard and yet have so little success.

We aren't stupid or ignorant, although oftentimes it was convenient to act that way. It was easier to pretend we didn't know how many calories were in the food we ate, or to come up with some foolish excuse for our overeating, rather than admit the truth that we couldn't stop.

We lied time and time again. We told you we were following the diets you prescribed when we weren't. You knew we were lying, and we knew that you knew. We also lied to ourselves, telling ourselves the same weak excuses for why we ate. Our denial was immense. We denied that we had a problem, and we were quite annoyed when, as part of your job, you told us we did.

Some of us have been afraid to visit you for fear of what you would say. We were so afraid of the infamous lecture that we stayed away entirely. Sometimes we put off routine care and let minor problems develop into crises.

We resented the medical profession. Some of us were traumatized by the thoughtless words of a doctor or nurse; others were told that there was no physical cause for our overeating and then handed a diet and shuffled off to a shrink. There probably is a physical cause, but we have not yet figured it out.

We were frustrated by the lack of a cure and blamed you, even though you tried your best. We may have vented our rage either to your face or behind your back. Many of us owe you amends for things we said. It must have been quite exasperating dealing with resentful patients like us, knowing that we were not going to follow your suggestions.

How to be most effective. So, given all of this, how can you be more effective for your patients who are overeaters? Be honest. You have a lot of authority, and hearing you describe the nature of an eating disorder and the need for a major life overhaul can have a great impact. Level with your patients and tell them what you know about the prognosis for their obesity. Tell them that the excess weight is a symptom of an eating disorder, and that as long as they continue to eat in their old way they will continue to be obese. A temporary diet plan won't fix them.

For those who are severe overeaters, you can recommend that they check out Overeaters Anonymous. It would be even more helpful if you could hand your patients a list of local meetings.* Recommend that they try several different meetings, because meetings vary, and it may take a little doing to find the right meeting for them. You could let them know that OA is inexpensive, but does require putting in a great deal of time.

Because OA isn't a diet club and doesn't endorse any food plans, it's likely that your patients will continue to seek nutritional advice and continued medical monitoring of their weight loss.

A final plea. After you have eliminated all known organic causes of overeating, please don't say there is nothing physically wrong with the patient. So little is understood about the biological basis for appetite that it's premature to say that there is nothing wrong. If you level with your patients and say that no one really knows what causes overeating, they will trust you and be more likely to follow the rest of your suggestions.

Furthermore, the future is likely to bring promising new treatments for overeating and obesity. Someday, there will be a cure. Consequently, your patients will probably come begging to you for the next potential miracle drug in this field. But please be cautious before using your patients as guinea pigs. Many other drugs were once touted as a cure, such as thyroid hormones and amphetamines, but were eventually found to be either unsafe or ineffective.

❧ To the researcher

I have a lot of faith that one day scientists will figure out the mysteries of the human appetite and find a cure for eating disorders. I try to stay current on the latest research, and I want to personally thank the dedicated sci-

---

*Most OA intergroups will gladly keep you up to date on local meetings. Just call or write them.

entists who are working so hard at trying to figure out what is going on and how to fix it.

Factor in OA participation. I would like to add a methodological note for those of you who are doing studies on human subjects. I have spent many hours reading the results of your research in journals like the *International Journal of Eating Disorders*. I have also met many people in Overeaters Anonymous who have been research subjects in these studies. And yet, it's extremely rare for a study to mention OA participation in any follow-ups. Given the size of OA, with 150,000 members attending ten thousand meetings in forty countries, it's highly likely that many of your subjects have been exposed to OA in one form or another.

Participation in OA may be a confounding variable that makes analysis of treatment results difficult. But any study of the effectiveness of various treatments for eating disorders should also attempt to factor in OA participation. It's easy to surmise that one type of treatment is more effective than another if many of the subjects in the first group are also in OA.

I can think of two competing hypotheses for the results of studying patients who are in OA: (1) OA attracts the "sickest of the sick"; such subjects would have the most intractable eating disorders and thus show a lower level of success than others whose eating disorders haven't progressed so far. (2) Regardless of the first hypothesis, participation in OA is so effective that you would find a success rate directly proportional to the frequency of OA attendance. After all, alcoholism professionals have known for years that active AA participation is one of the best ways to stay sober.

I would like to invite you to research the OA program. The alcoholism literature contains many references to AA, yet the eating disorder literature contains few references to OA. There is a dearth of serious scholarship into the program.

Of course, doing a double-blind, placebo-controlled study on an OA participant is virtually impossible. The fact that we don't keep any meaningful records on members makes long-term follow-up extremely difficult. But at the very least researchers should be aware that their subjects have been exposed to OA, and should attempt to account for this in the analysis of their results.

Since OA is one possible treatment for eating disorders, professionals should be aware of this, and it should be mentioned in books that discuss treatment methodologies. However, the practitioner dealing with eating-disordered patients needs to know which treatments work best for which patients. Studies aimed at the kind of people who do best in OA would be of great interest.

Even studies that describe the OA treatment process in a manner that informs fellow researchers of the strengths and weaknesses of OA would be useful. From time to time, OA surveys its members; professional interpretation of the results would be helpful.

Of course, any study that uses OA members should also look at their degree of OA participation. There appears to be a big difference in recovery rates between those members who only go to a meeting every few weeks and those who go to several meetings a week, perform service for the group, and have frequent contact with other OA members.

Little has been published about the medical complications of the formerly obese. In the past, this was quite understandable because there have been so few people with long-term maintenance of large weight loss. But most of us who were obese know that some of the damage we have done to ourselves may be permanent, and we wonder what we should watch for. We know about the stretch marks, loose skin, and cold hands, but what else is there? A lot of us are curious.

Afterword:
A daily reprieve

Writing this book has taken me several years. Although I have learned a lot during this time, I am sure that I will learn even more over the years to come. I know that more will be revealed. The authors of *Alcoholics Anonymous* must have felt the same way; on the final page of the first section of that magnificent work they wrote, "We realize we know only a little."[*]

Yes, we know only a little. There is so much that we don't know about eating disorders, about the inner workings of the brain, and about the mysteries of spiritual development. A great deal more needs to be learned.

But I already know some things. I know I am not cured. Even though it has been over ten years since my last binge, I know there is no guarantee that I won't go out and start bingeing tomorrow. I have observed other overeaters who thought they were cured and yet had major relapses. All we get is a daily reprieve, contingent on maintaining a fit spiritual condition.

As anyone who has ever kept off a lot of weight will tell you, maintenance takes much effort and requires major changes, not only changes in eating habits but in thinking habits. I firmly believe that whatever was wrong with my appetite will continue to malfunction for the rest of my life. Thus, I need to continue to do the things that I have been doing to keep from overeating.

There is no graduation from an eating disorder. It's a seductive thought to pretend that we are cured and that we can have just one bite of those old

---

[*] *Alcoholics Anonymous,* 164.

binge foods now and then. I love the analogy of dialysis—like dialysis, abstinence must be continued indefinitely. By reaching outside myself to other overeaters, I somehow get the reminders, the reinforcement, and the support that keep me from destructive overeating, one day at a time.

Another good analogy is that of brushing and flossing your teeth. If you want your teeth to be healthy and sparkle, you need to brush and floss them regularly. Sure, you can get by for a few days without doing it, but the consequences are unpleasant. You lose that clean feeling that comes from taking care of yourself. Your breath sours and your teeth look bad. As the plaque and tartar build up, bacteria find a home and gum disease gets started, resulting in serious dental problems that cost a lot of money and may never be fully repaired.

It's much the same way with the OA tools. Sure, I can go for a while without using them, but gradually that calm, serene, and clean feeling gets replaced by craziness and anxiety, and sooner or later overeating starts to look good. By sharing what I have learned with other overeaters, I continue to get that daily reprieve.

Writing is one of these tools, and writing this book has done me a great deal of good. It has forced me to think hard about OA and how it works—to be observant about what works and what doesn't. I've learned that what really works is trying to help another overeater.

At this point, it's good to remember the story of Ebby. Ebby was one of the founders of AA—the sober man who reached out to Bill W. and said, "I've got religion."* He also had a part in the publishing of the original edition of *Alcoholics Anonymous.* But Ebby ended up drinking again. The folklore within the fellowship says that he didn't continue to do enough work with other alcoholics. I realize that just writing this book provides no guarantee. I can't rest on my laurels. The only way to coast is downhill. But to paraphrase AA cofounder Dr. Bob, who was sober for the rest of his life despite severe cravings, as long as I think the way I think today, and do the things that I do today, I am convinced that I never have to overeat again.†

You may not agree with everything you read in this book. I don't expect you to. Take what you need and leave the rest. This book is my best effort at distilling into print what I have learned in OA. It doesn't represent the views of OA, only my own, and I reserve the right to change them. I could probably make the same remark about this book that the famous economist F. M. Scherer made about one of his books: "Half of this book is wrong, but I don't know which half."

My goal is to revise this book as I progress in my own recovery and as we learn more within OA about how to recover. If you have any comments or suggestions, please send them to me in care of the publisher.

---

* *Alcoholics Anonymous,* 9.
† *Alcoholics Anonymous,* 206.

The Twelve Steps of Alcoholics Anonymous*

1. We admitted we were powerless over alcohol—that our lives had become unmanageable.

2. Came to believe that a Power greater than ourselves could restore us to sanity.

3. Made a decision to turn our will and our lives over to the care of God *as we understood Him.*

4. Made a searching and fearless moral inventory of ourselves.

5. Admitted to God, to ourselves, and to another human being the exact nature of our wrongs.

6. Were entirely ready to have God remove all these defects of character.

7. Humbly asked Him to remove our shortcomings.

8. Made a list of all persons we had harmed, and became willing to make amends to them all.

9. Made direct amends to such people wherever possible, except when to do so would injure them or others.

10. Continued to take personal inventory and when we were wrong promptly admitted it.

11. Sought through prayer and meditation to improve our conscious contact with God *as we understood Him,* praying only for knowledge of His will for us and the power to carry that out.

12. Having had a spiritual awakening as the result of these steps, we tried to carry this message to alcoholics, and to practice these principles in all our affairs.

---

*The Twelve Steps of Alcoholics Anonymous are taken from *Alcoholics Anonymous,* 3d ed., published by AA World Services, Inc., New York, N.Y., 59-60. Reprinted with permission of AA World Services, Inc. (See editor's note on copyright page.)

The Twelve Traditions of Alcoholics Anonymous*

1. Our common welfare should come first; personal recovery depends upon A.A. unity.

2. For our group purpose there is but one ultimate authority—a loving God as He may express Himself in our group conscience. Our leaders are but trusted servants; they do not govern.

3. The only requirement for A.A. membership is a desire to stop drinking.

4. Each group should be autonomous except in matters affecting other groups or A.A. as a whole.

5. Each group has but one primary purpose—to carry its message to the alcoholic who still suffers.

6. An A.A. group ought never endorse, finance or lend the A.A. name to any related facility or outside enterprise, lest problems of money, property and prestige divert us from our primary purpose.

7. Every A.A. group ought to be fully self-supporting, declining outside contributions.

8. Alcoholics Anonymous should remain forever nonprofessional, but our service centers may employ special workers.

9. A.A., as such, ought never to be organized; but we may create service boards or committees directly responsible to those they serve.

10. Alcoholics Anonymous has no opinion on outside issues; hence the A.A. name ought never be drawn into public controversy.

11. Our public relations policy is based on attraction rather than promotion; we need always maintain personal anonymity at the level of press, radio and films.

12. Anonymity is the spiritual foundation of all our Traditions, ever reminding us to place principles before personalities.

The Twelve Steps of Overeaters Anonymous*

1. We admitted we were powerless over food—that our lives had become unmanageable.

2. Came to believe that a Power greater than ourselves could restore us to sanity.

3. Made a decision to turn our will and our lives over to the care of God *as we understood Him.*

4. Made a searching and fearless moral inventory of ourselves.

5. Admitted to God, to ourselves, and to another human being the exact nature of our wrongs.

6. Were entirely ready to have God remove all these defects of character.

7. Humbly asked Him to remove our shortcomings.

8. Made a list of all persons we had harmed and became willing to make amends to them all.

9. Made direct amends to such people wherever possible, except when to do so would injure them or others.

10. Continued to take personal inventory and when we were wrong, promptly admitted it.

11. Sought through prayer and meditation to improve our conscious contact with God *as we understood Him,* praying only for knowledge of His will for us and the power to carry that out.

12. Having had a spiritual awakening as the result of these steps, we tried to carry this message to compulsive overeaters and to practice these principles in all our affairs.

The Twelve Traditions of Overeaters Anonymous*

1. Our common welfare should come first; personal recovery depends upon OA unity.

2. For our group purpose there is but one ultimate authority—a loving God as He may express Himself in our group conscience. Our leaders are but trusted servants; they do not govern.

3. The only requirement for OA membership is a desire to stop eating compulsively.

4. Each group should be autonomous except in matters affecting other groups or OA as a whole.

5. Each group has but one primary purpose—to carry its message to the compulsive overeater who still suffers.

6. An OA group ought never endorse, finance, or lend the OA name to any related facility or outside enterprise, lest problems of money, property, and prestige divert us from our primary purpose.

7. Every OA group ought to be fully self-supporting, declining outside contributions.

8. Overeaters Anonymous should remain forever nonprofessional, but our service centers may employ special workers.

9. OA, as such, ought never be organized; but we may create service boards or committees directly responsible to those they serve.

10. Overeaters Anonymous has no opinion on outside issues; hence the OA name ought never be drawn into public controversy.

11. Our public relations policy is based on attraction rather than promotion; we need always maintain personal anonymity at the level of press, radio, films, television, and other public media of communication.

12. Anonymity is the spiritual foundation of all these traditions, ever reminding us to place principles before personalities.

---

*Permission to use the Twelve Traditions of Alcoholics Anonymous for adaptation granted to Overeaters Anonymous by AA World Services, Inc. The Twelve Traditions of Overeaters Anonymous, as adapted, are reprinted here with the permission of Overeaters Anonymous, Inc. (See editor's note on copyright page.)

Glossary

Just as trades or professions develop jargon, so does Overeaters Anonymous. This glossary explains some of the phrases that you may hear in the fellowship.

ABSTINENCE. Abstaining from compulsive overeating. A form of rational eating that accords with the food discipline appropriate for each person; often modified with adjectives such as "clean" or "sloppy." A losing abstinence is one in which a person is intending to lose weight.

ACA OR ACOA. Adult Children of Alcoholics. Sometimes used to refer to a person who is the offspring of an alcoholic; other times used to refer to Al-Anon meetings that specialize in ACAs or groups that aren't Al-Anon-affiliated.

AL-ANON. A self-help group for the friends and family members of alcoholics that uses the Twelve Steps of AA.

AMENDS. The process of repairing harm done to others as called for in Steps Nine and Ten.

ANONYMITY. A concept of respect for the privacy of the individual. It's often said at meetings, "Who you see here, what you hear here, let it stay here." It's up to the individual member to decide whether, and to whom, to reveal his or her OA membership. Also, members don't publicly reveal their affiliation with the program.

ANOREXIA NERVOSA. An eating disorder related to but different from compulsive overeating that causes the victim to restrict his or her food intake to the point of becoming dangerously underweight.

AWOL GROUPS. A Way Of Life Groups. Many overeaters have formed closed groups strictly to work the Twelve Steps. Since these groups have specific starting and stopping dates, as well as other rules on attendance and abstinence, they aren't OA groups as such. But many OA members attend such groups for assistance in working the Steps.

BIG BOOK. The book *Alcoholics Anonymous,* published by AA.

BILL W. A New York stockbroker and one of the cofounders of Alcoholics Anonymous. Bill W. wrote much of the AA literature, including major portions of the Big Book and *Twelve Steps and Twelve Traditions.*

BLUE SHEET. An old food plan of OA that was once printed on a blue sheet of paper. It was similar to the old Gray Sheet food plan.

BULIMAREXIA. An eating disorder in which the victim consumes large quantities of food, as in bulimia, but also purges and starves to the point of severe emaciation, as in anorexia.

BULIMIA. An eating disorder in which the victim consumes large quantities of food and often vomits or uses laxatives to get rid of it.

CODEPENDENT. A friend, relative, or acquaintance of an addict who becomes obsessed with attempting to control the addict's behavior.

CROSSTALK. Interrupting, blurting out, or speaking out of turn at a meeting. Frowned upon in OA.

DIGNITY OF CHOICE. The last set of food plans ever published by OA; withdrawn in 1986.

DR. BOB. An Akron, Ohio, surgeon who was one of the AA cofounders.

EATING DISORDER UNIT (EDU). A residential treatment center for eating disorders that provides inpatient care. Often associated with other drug and alcohol rehabilitation programs.

FAT SERENITY. Gaining emotional peace but not recovering physically.

FOOD PLAN. A method of eating. To some people it's a euphemism for a diet. The word *diet* is rarely used by OA members because it usually refers to some temporary, gimmicky way of eating that is designed for the sole purpose of losing weight.

FOOD THOUGHT. An unwanted thought about food that may involve the desire to eat inappropriately or irrationally.

GRAY SHEET. An old low-carbohydrate food plan of OA printed on a gray sheet of paper and sometimes referred to as Plan A. It was later known as Plan Number 3 in The Dignity of Choice. The Gray Sheet allowed three weighed and measured meals a day consisting mostly of vegetables and protein with a little fruit.

GROUP CONSCIENCE. The consensus of the group. There are no leaders who make major decisions, either for the individual group or the fellowship as a whole. Each group relies on a democratic consensus when making decisions. After all, 150,000 heads are better than one.

HALT. An acronym for the slogan "Don't get too Hungry, Angry, Lonely, or Tired."

H.O.W. GROUPS. Honesty, Openmindedness, and Willingness Groups are much more rigidly structured than regular OA meetings. Such groups, which are quite controversial within OA, sometimes push specific food plans, such as modified forms of the Gray Sheet.

HUNDRED-POUNDERS MEETING. A meeting specifically designed for those who have been morbidly obese (one hundred pounds or more overweight). Also known as "century meetings."

INTERGROUP. A group consisting of representatives from several OA groups in an area. An intergroup usually handles things like meeting lists and telephone answering services at the county or state level. An intergroup also sends delegates to regional and World Service Business Conferences.

LETTING GO. The act of accepting the way things are, and thus gaining peace of mind. For example, "I just had to let go of the fact that I didn't get the job I wanted." A common slogan is "Let Go and Let God."

LIFELINE. A monthly magazine published by the World Service Office. Annual subscriptions are $12.99 per year

MARATHON. A daylong series of meetings, usually organized as a special event.

O-ANON. An organization for the friends and families of compulsive overeaters, patterned after Al-Anon. O-Anon meetings tend to be few and far between.

OLD TAPES. Old ways of thinking and acting that are now inappropriate. For example, "I felt like eating after that job interview, but that was just an old tape."

ORANGE SHEET. Another early food plan named after the color of paper it was printed on. Unlike the Gray Sheet, this food plan included bread.

PINK CLOUD. An early stage in recovery in which abstaining from overeating seems effortless.

PROMISES. A passage from pages 83–84 of *Alcoholics Anonymous* that is sometimes read at the end of meetings. It's called the "Promises" because it lists the good things that happen as a result of working the Steps.

QUALIFY. Telling one's story at a meeting, as in "I qualified at the noon meeting yesterday."

RECOVERY. The process of repairing the physical, emotional, and spiritual damage of compulsive overeating.

REGION. The OA service body that handles affairs for larger geographic areas than intergroups. There are currently nine regions wordwide.

RELAPSE. A return to compulsive overeating that is of much greater severity than a slip.

ROZANNE S. The Los Angeles woman who founded OA in 1960.

SERENITY PRAYER. A simple prayer that is often said at the beginning of OA meetings.

SERVICE. Any action that helps carry the OA message to others. This includes setting up chairs at meetings and giving rides to others, as well as more formal duties, such as being group secretary.

SEVENTH TRADITION. "Every OA group ought to be fully self-supporting, declining outside contributions." OA doesn't solicit or accept donations from outsiders, and yet there are no dues or fees. A basket is usually passed at meetings to cover each group's expenses. Often the basket or the money itself is referred to as the Seventh Tradition.

SHORTSTOP MEETING. A meeting that is only one hour long.

SLIP. A slight mistake in eating that is less severe than a relapse.

SPONSOR. An OA member who helps lead another OA member through the program. Many people ask a sponsor to advise them on specific parts of the program, such as dealing with food, working the Steps, or maintenance.

STEERING MEETING. A short meeting, usually held right after or before a regular OA meeting, in which business items are discussed. Attendance is open to anyone. Called a "business" or "group conscience" meeting in some areas.

STEPS. The Twelve Steps of the OA program, which are patterned after the Twelve Steps of AA.

SURRENDER. The act of accepting the world as it is and taking the actions necessary to deal with it. We often speak of "surrendering" to the program.

THIRTEENTH-STEPPING. Getting romantically involved with another OA member.

TOOLS. Actions that we have found are essential to our recovery: abstinence, meetings, sponsorship, literature, telephone calls, anonymity, writing, and service.

TRADITIONS. The Twelve Traditions of OA. Patterned after the Twelve Traditions of AA, these govern how the individual groups function.

TURNING IT OVER. Similar to letting go. Turning it over involves asking God for help and guidance. For example, "I couldn't let go of my resentment until I turned it over."

TWELFTH STEP. As a verb, to let someone know about OA.

TWELVE AND TWELVE. The book *Twelve Steps and Twelve Traditions,* published by AA, which contains a detailed discussion of the Steps and Traditions of the AA program.

WORLD SERVICE BUSINESS CONFERENCE. Sometimes called "Conference." An organizational body that meets yearly in Los Angeles, consisting of delegates from OA groups around the world. The Conference oversees the World Service Office and acts as the group conscience for OA as a whole.

WSO. The World Service Office of Overeaters Anonymous. Handles administrative matters for all of OA. WSO prints and distributes the literature, publishes *Lifeline* magazine, assists local groups, and maintains a listing of all OA groups in the world.

Index

About the author

Jim A. went on his first diet at the age of ten, his first battle in a lifelong struggle with obesity. Taking a geographic cure by moving from Pennsylvania to California didn't solve his food and weight problems, nor did an endless array of diets and exercise schemes, including a stint on his college football team.

He waddled into Overeaters Anonymous in 1981 and by the spring of 1982 was 110 pounds lighter, a weight that he has maintained ever since. He has been active at all levels of OA, including delegate to Regional and World Business Conferences. He is the founder of the first OA computer bulletin board system, the OAsis. He has also published several articles in *Lifeline*, the monthly magazine of OA. Over the years he has attended over two thousand OA meetings.

Jim has a Ph.D. in finance and teaches at a well-known university. In addition to books and computers, he enjoys bicycling and hiking. Jim lives with his wife Amy and daughter Betsy near Washington, D.C.

Other titles to support recovery . . .

Meditations for Dieters and Overeaters
Meditations from *Food for Thought* and *Inner Harvest*
> *by Elisabeth L.*

Accentuate the positives of Twelve Step recovery from compulsive eating disorders with these four topical meditation booklets. Each includes 30 meditations that focus on an issue often raised in recovery.

Order No. 1487 Finding Motivation
Order No. 1486 Kindness to Ourselves
Order No. 1484 Making Good Decisions
Order No. 1485 A New Body Image

Body and Soul
A Guide to Lasting Recovery from Compulsive Eating and Bulimia
> *by Susan Meltsner, M.S.W.*

What triggers overeating? For those of us discovering a new life in recovery, dealing with the causes—the thoughts and events that trigger our destructive behavior—is the key to to handling life's challenges. Think of this book as a survival kit intended to help us through each new day. 240 pp.
Order No. 5098

Hope for Compulsive Eaters
> *from Judi Hollis, Ph.D.*

Twelve audio cassettes address the problems—and the solutions—those of us with eating disorders most often confront. From one of the nation's leading eating disorder experts comes thoughtful, practical advice about family dynamics, fear of success, assertiveness training, gentle eating, and more. 60 minutes each.
Order No. 5650

**For price and order information, or a free catalog, please
call our Telephone Representatives**
HAZELDEN EDUCATIONAL MATERIALS
1-800-328-9000   **1-612-257-4010**   **1-612-257-1331**
(Toll Free. U.S., Canada   (Outside the U.S. & Canada)   (24-Hour FAX)
& the Virgin Islands)

Pleasant Valley Road • P.O. Box 176 • Center City, MN 55012-0176

Hazelden Europe • PO Box 616 • Cork, Ireland
Int'l Access Code+353-21-314318
FAX: Int'l Access Code+353-21-961269